Unsearchable Riches:

The Symbolic Nature of Liturgy

David N. Power, O.M.I.

Unsearchable Riches:
The
Symbolic Nature of Liturgy

Pueblo Publishing Company

New York

Design: Frank Kacmarcik

Scriptural pericopes from the Revised Standard Version.

ISBN: 0-916134-62-8

Printed in the United States of America.

Contents

Preface

As author, I see something a trifle absurd about writing
a book which relates studies on symbol to an
understanding of Christian liturgy. The literature on
both topics is so vast and the issues so complicated that
survey and synthesis are both impossible. Yet I have
yielded to the pressure of friends, colleagues, and
students and prepared this work. The pressure arose as
the result of a modest attempt a decade ago to survey
some important works on symbol for the English
review *The Way*. This survey appeared as four articles
in 1972, 1973, and 1974. Since then it seems to have
been often cited, used in classes, and mentioned in
bibliographies. I have been asked frequently to publish
these articles in book form. The Reverend James Walsh,
S.J., editor of *The Way*, has been kind enough to allow
me to make whatever use I wish of the articles.

In fact very little is taken directly from these articles
and this is effectively a new work, which I hope is
more coherent and pursues issues further, while
retaining the usefulness that was apparently found in
the original survey. No claim is made to give a
complete account of studies that have been done or of
questions that merit discussion. My desire is more
precisely to offer room for thought and to allure those
who wish to think more deeply about liturgy and its
symbolic nature, knowing full well that they may
disagree with me on some points and find my work
inadequate on others.

I have adopted a particular plan and purpose in composing the work. The purpose might be said to show the need for the crisis of the religious imagination in liturgical participation and understanding, as well as the need to relate the study and practice of liturgy to culture and culture's critical development. The plan is to start with an awareness of symbolic crisis in liturgical celebration and to offer insight into it and its resolution by discussing the many forms of expression included under the broad umbrella of the word *symbol*.

It will be clear that a few particular authors have had a major impact on my thought. I do not pretend to give perfect insight into their work, but simply recognize my debt to them and offer apologies to them and to the readers for distortions. It would be meritorious to offer a good and full bibliography on the topics of the book, but such is well nigh beyond human range. In the bibliography at the end of the book, my choice has been to list only those works that have occurred in the notes. I trust that whatever books and articles are listed will in themselves be sufficient invitation to the curious reader to look even further.

Besides thanking James Walsh, for reasons already mentioned, I wish to thank Bernard Benziger of Pueblo Publishing Company for undertaking to publish this work, and Kevin McLaughlin, also of Pueblo, who did the copy editing. Michael Downey, Kenneth Hannon, Stephen Happel, and William Marravee all read the original manuscript and offered helpful suggestions and encouragement. I thank them as both colleagues and friends. I am also grateful to James Garneau who helped compile the index. Lastly, I cannot refrain from mentioning the many students who over the course of the years, in Ireland, in Rome, and in Washington, have provided occasion, instigation, and inspiration for research and thought in the area covered by this book.

David Noel Power, O.M.I.   *May 6, 1983*
The Catholic University of America
Washington, D.C.

Introduction

This study has two aims. The first is to relate studies on symbolism and its modes to an understanding of the liturgy. The second is to relate these studies to the renewal of the liturgy in a time of crisis. Since the first aim is affected by the second, it may be well to say something about the nature of the crisis at this point, although it will be more fully treated in the first chapter.

The crisis as it touches on liturgy is twofold. First there is a crisis of vision and second a crisis of hope. The churches are forced to ask how well the vision of reality, or the world view, projected in liturgical celebration expresses a sense of being in time and a sense of the holy that are pertinent to contemporary fact and contemporary models of reality. This is the crisis of vision. At the same time, the churches are part of a humanity which lives in a time of disintegration and destruction, a humanity continually compelled to consider whether there are any hopes by which it is possible to face the future. The despair of the age is represented in the twofold holocaust of the century. There is the holocaust of the Jewish people under the Nazi regime, and there is the imminent nuclear holocaust which threatens the entire world. Can those who profess faith in Jesus Christ profess it in such an age?

Because this is an ever-present issue for worship, a work such as this one is engaged throughout not only in explanation but also in interpretation, interpretation of the past and of the future. In liturgical studies, it is certainly necessary to recover the past. This was the avowed aim of the members of the Second Vatican Council, and it has been the aim of much study that has influenced the changes in the liturgy that have taken place since, not only in the Roman Catholic Church but in other churches as well. In looking to the past, however, interpretation cannot be content to recover texts and rituals, or the surplus of the cultural and historical to which they belong. It must look as well to what has been neglected, to what has been forgotten, and to what has been distorted in the life of the church and in the confession of faith that worship embodies. This is explained more fully in a later chapter, but needs to be kept in mind from the beginning.

Interpretation also looks to the future, out of the encounter with history and its appropriation. An interpretative formulation of hopes for the future is possible on condition that we are able to articulate before God our own experience of history and the world, our current sense of the presence and absence of God. The greatest temptation threatening liturgical reform is that of a retreat into the past, or of a retreat into abstract universalism, a temptation to which the churches would succumb were they to remain silent before the twofold holocaust, to refuse to address it in their common worship. Faced by this need, the understanding of the role in worship of such actions as narrative and lament is vital, and is an integral part of this present work.

The first chapter is addressed then to an explanation of the liturgical crisis that occurs within the greater crisis, with particular attention to how this affects our understanding of the symbolic character of liturgy. This chapter is complemented by a second which gives a

2

historical perspective on how the symbolic has been lived and explained in the past. This gives us some idea of where we are coming from and what may be recovered from history.

The next three chapters relate more general symbolic studies to an understanding of liturgy, investigating what might be termed the components of the symbolic. They explain how fresh understandings of the bodily, of ritual, of verbal images, of myth, narrative, and modes of prayer illuminate the ways in which such elements converge to construct the whole that is referred to as liturgy, or common and ecclesial worship.

Chapter 6 uses these explanations to present the liturgy as the mystery of the church and the mystery in which God is made manifest in the remembrance of Jesus Christ by the community of faith. It explores the essential structures of worship, or the ways in which the symbolic in its various forms is integrated into the church's celebration of its own mystery and of the mystery of salvation.

Chapter 7 is ontological in intent. It approaches ontological issues from the standpoint of the symbolic. First, it explains how the liturgy constitutes humanity's self-expression. Second, it explains how the liturgy may be seen as the manifestation of God's being in the world and of humanity's being in God. Some conclusions are drawn in the final part of the book relating to the resolution of the twofold crisis with which the work begins.

If one were to ask whether this work develops a model for the interpretation of the liturgy, the answer would be that it offers a transformational model. In other words, the fundamental understanding of liturgy and sacrament is that when they are celebrated as acts of faith they transform human experience. This they do by bringing it to expression and thus relating it to the memory of Jesus Christ and to his presence in the church through the Spirit. The model is in the first place heuristic. Since much attention is given to the forms of symbolic expression used in worship, it offers ways of interpreting what is expressed and what takes place in the community when it celebrates. The model is also ontological, in a twofold sense. First, it offers insight into the nature of humanity's coming to be through liturgical memorial. Second, it represents liturgy as the mode of God's coming to be in the church and as a revelation of divine presence in the world. The model gives insight into the historical nature of the church's worship. Not only does it change in the course of history, in relation to different cultural expressions, but it must change in order to continue to express the meaning of God's presence in history and of history's redemption in God. In coming to an awareness of itself as sacrament of God's reign, the church continues to mediate the transformation of new realities and experiences.

Chapter One

The State of Liturgy: Symbolic Crisis

The purpose of this work is to explore the symbolic
nature of liturgy, but in what context is that being
done? We know that enormous changes are being
effected in common worship in all the Christian
churches, yet we are often left with the feeling that
they do not offer us a receivable sense of reality or a
refined sense of the holy. It is suggested in this chapter
that this has to do not merely with a lack of empathy
with the imaginary and the symbolic, but more deeply
with the vision of reality that is often projected in
worship. Do common and accepted modes of liturgical
expression respond adequately to contemporary ways
of perceiving and being, and do they allow for hope in
the future when we are threatened with awesome
destruction?

It may be useful to set out in schematic form what is
done in this introductory chapter. The steps taken are
as follows:

1. It is explained how the symbolic belongs to the
public forum of life lived in society and community.
Also explained is what goes on when a group of people
need to reshape their myths and symbols in order to
engage meaningfully in new experiences.

2. The particular problems of the hierarchical or
classical vision of the world that is the more immediate
heritage of Western worship are then explored, so that

it may be clear how the churches are engaged in something more fundamental than a historical retrieval or a fostering of the symbolic sense of their participants.

3. It is explained how the development of society and human knowledge has led to a differentiated mode of expression, so that today we distinguish between the every-day, the mythical, and the scientific. It is necessary to see how this differentiation affects liturgical expression.

4. The points mentioned above leave humanity and the churches in a position in which there is a clash of world views and a clash of ways in which reality is perceived and expressed. This also entails a clash of ways in which people want to face the future, live in hope and construct a world in which to live. The nature of this disharmony and its consequences for liturgy are discussed.

5. World views must deal with suffering, but they do so in a variety of ways, some of which offer privilege to the few and add to the oppression of others. The churches are increasingly aware of their prophetic role in society, of their commitment to the poor, and of the ministry of reconciliation to which they are called in a world of increasing violence. This has to be reflected in the ways in which God's mystery is expressed in liturgy.

6. A model is suggested within which the symbolic may construct a vision of reality, one which serves the need to integrate new experience and to look in faith and hope to the future. It is one in which the temporal prevails over the topological and which allows for the creativity of the aesthetic imagination.

These explorations of crisis will make it more obvious why and in what sense it is pertinent to examine the symbolic nature of liturgy and the different modes of expression that are included under that general rubric.

SOCIETIES AND THEIR SYMBOLS

The law is overused in contemporary Western society. Recent court cases have decided the rights of grandparents to see their grandchildren in the instance of the divorce of the childrens' parents. Natural instinct and a cultural appreciation of kinship no longer seem to suffice. While industrial companies pollute rivers and the air, citizens have no defense other than an appeal to the courts or a request for new laws. There is apparently no feeling for harmony between nature and human dwelling to constitute a common bond between dwellers and users.

The law intervenes where cultural traditions of social significance are transgressed, or where such traditions no longer capture the common imagination or provide meaningful standards for human conduct. It has become commonplace in studies on symbol to underline their necessity in a society's pursuit of meaningful existence. The individual functions freely when inspired by symbols, and society finds coherence in those that are held in public esteem. In times of tremendous social upheaval it is normal for the symbolic tradition to lose some of its credibility and adherence, for the simple reason that its systemic presentation relates to social realities that are in flux or have already been left behind. The reverse is the case when the loss of credibility in symbolic language is at least partially responsible for social change. In either situation, social coherence and a sense of common meaning are bound to beliefs and persuasions that are articulated in symbolic form. The ultimate value of a society's cultural tradition lies in the ability to articulate it anew in ways pertinent to new historical realities.

Some decades ago, in *Philosophy in a New Key*, Susanne K. Langer wrote: "A mind that is oriented, no matter by what conscious or unconscious symbols, in material and social realities, can function freely and confidently even under great pressure of circumstance and in the face of hard problems,"[1] while at the same time, saying of our contemporary Western experience, that ". . . our intelligence is keen but precarious: it lacks metaphysical myth, régime, and ritual expression."[2]

Pointing to the importance of symbols of life, death, sin, and salvation, she felt that Christianity could no longer furnish the symbols or the wholeness needed. On the one hand, Langer believed that Christianity is tied to a mythological view of the cosmos that is alien to technology, technology's advances, and the technological mind which is typical of contemporary persons and society. On the other hand, attributing great importance—for freedom and society's well-being—to art and aesthetic expression, she feared that church leaders had abandoned all sense of beauty in religious expression and in the environment of religious ritual. In the event of the failure of this traditional world view, therefore, Langer did not look for a revival of religion, but espoused the view that society should look for wholeness in persons whose life could be called "a ritual performance"[3] in favor of a cause, and to artists who try to express the meaning of life by re-creating a tradition, which in the process undergoes some vast and extraordinary shift in its transmission. To be able to re-create this tradition in aesthetic forms means that one is gifted with interiority, with personal freedom and creative power, and with the ability to perceive a human society in tune with nature and the cosmos, without having to resort to the alienated cosmology which Langer ascribed to Christianity. Despite massive trends to cede freedom to organization, nature to technology, and the cosmos to exploration,

Langer believed that the human spirit was able to survive and to create a free and humane society around the symbols that could be given persuasive force through free action and aesthetic expression.

In the face of social and cultural collapse, it is quite common to look to artists for direction. In his vast work on the masks of God, Joseph Campbell writes of a tradition which forced the journey inward and which remained alive even in periods when hierarchical systems seemed to reduce its voice to a whisper.[4] It was a voice which he heard speaking for personal freedom and an inner sense of meaning, even in periods of history or in cultural epochs when public systems were so vigorous that the voice of individuals acting out of personal consciousness seemed unimportant. For him as for many others an artist such as James Joyce, in his flight for freedom and away from the fetters of nation, family, and religion, can remain a type of the contemporary experience that leads the human person to search for new worlds to inhabit, for the power to create in freedom from all bonds of external pressure, even while delving constantly into the past, looking there for the secret betrayed by society or by church. Every person aware of personal freedom and creativity, or of the need for interiority, could say: "I go to encounter for the millionth time the reality of experience and to forge in the smithy of my soul the uncreated conscience of my race."[5]

CULTURAL DISSONANCE AND LITURGY
This appeal to interiority, to personal creative freedom, to the aesthetic powers of artists goes along with a perception of cultural and religious upheaval described in the image of the broken center that we owe to the poet William Butler Yeats.[6] This is an appropriate image to describe the collapse of traditional premises regarding the radical significance of things, the absence

9

of any robust common faith, the turning of basic cultural presuppositions into yawning question marks.[7] In the face of the multiple decadence of cultural, social, and political systems across the globe, it is commonly recognized that survival and revival are possible only on the basis of newly emerging symbolic coherence. It is worth reflecting on some concrete analyses of this situation, in order to perceive the better what issues are at stake in the renewal of liturgy as a symbol system, and also perhaps to understand why too cerebral and organizational an approach to liturgical change has not borne the fruits apparently intended.

A first example is the development of the Irish nation since its independence in 1921.[8] When the Irish people became a free nation in that year, efforts made in preceding decades to express a national identity were given state and ecclesiastical approval and support. The heritage of the Celt, the Gaelic language, and the Catholic faith were heralded. The inauthenticity of this cluster of symbols or myths has much to do with current problems in that country. The effort to symbolize the national identity was too wedded to these fictions, and too accommodating to an economically and culturally conservative tendency, to be of great hold in the Ireland that some decades later started to look for its place among the commonwealth of nations and to share in the affluence that technology promised. In fact, Ireland is not made up of Celts, its language is its own peculiar ways with English, and its faith is not confined within the boundaries of the Roman Catholic Church. In face of this dissolution of what had been proposed as a cultural center, Terence Brown writes of the need that ". . . in future a new humanely comprehensive ideological imperative be defined for Irish society—one which would take account of the material and social gains of modernization but which would also allow a sustaining and challenging role for the products of the imagination and of the mind."[9]

Like the authors already mentioned, Brown believes that the function of providing this sense of identity, and the forms and symbols in which it is given expression, belongs to artists. A general lack of artists, poets, and writers who are willing to tackle the issue of cultural identity leaves him pessimistic about the future. His reflection on the ideology or mythology[10] that expresses a common identity and cultural coherence points up two factors that are useful to underline. First, the ideology has to be adequate or authentic. That is to say, it must account for the real facts, however it wishes to direct them or give them meaning. An expression of identity that ignores the real composition of a people, or that is innocent of social and economic possibilities, may be at least the partial cause of a good deal of public and social strife. It will not be a source of cohesion and fulfillment. Second, the discovery of an adequate ideology and the creation of apt modes of its expression has the characteristics of the intuitive. It is not susceptible to planning and organization, but is supplied by those minds that from within their hearts look to tradition and history, and are not afraid to project a future that catches the imagination of real rather than fictitious people.

Looking at other parts of the globe, and from a perspective different from that of the historian, the anthropologist Clifford Geertz has given a good deal of consideration to what happens to the political life of countries in Asia and Africa when contact with the Western world brings about upheaval of their present systems.[11] He points out that in many of these countries, the exercise and distribution of power worked very well according to traditional patterns until external forces and ideas changed the social systems and needs that were served by these patterns. Economic facts and possibilities were altered and dwelling habits could no longer remain the same. Ironically, it is as Geertz remarks "in country unfamiliar emotionally or topographically that one needs poems and road maps,"[12] and coherent cultural symbols seem to be most lacking when they are most needed. Change in relations to cosmos and bios cannot be peacefully negotiated, however, without change in cultural symbol and ideology. One looks to these countries to see how artistic creation and imaginative leadership will respond to the new feelings about identity and relationships.

This brief introductory reflection on symbol systems and their place in an evolving society can alert one to what is at stake in liturgical change, or to the issues that made change necessary, however well or badly enforced. There were doubtless many motives and pressures which caused the bishops at the Second Vatican Council to decree a reform of the liturgy and to eventually make provisions for the use of the vernacular. John XXIII had called for an *aggiornamento*. This allowed for a distinction between substance and accident which seemed to find a first instance of implementation in worship, where the bishops were accustomed to a distinction between what was essential to sacraments (matter and form) and what was accidental or secondary. There were also the pressures of the liturgical movement, which for decades had been promoting greater participation of the laity in liturgy. This was based on a view of the church taken from early tradition, where it was seen as the community of the baptized, this community being the actor in the liturgy. This kind of ecclesiology was given explicit form after the constitution on the liturgy was accepted, but it is implicit in the changes proposed for liturgical reform.

In some respects, the Second Vatican Council did not come to grips with its fundamental mission until near the end of its life, when it turned to the relation between church and world, from which there followed the constitution on the church in the world. Advertence to this relationship is almost absent from the document on the liturgy, and this is a weakness which has dogged the liturgical reforms ever since.[13] There has not been enough consideration given to cultural patterns, enough awareness that changes in forms of worship affect deeply rooted cultural beliefs and emotions, enough thought given to what effect social and economic change has on the place that religious expression has among peoples. From a purely ecclesiological perspective, not enough attention has been given in the reforms of the liturgical books to the difference between a hierarchical vision of the church and a communitarian one, nor has there been enough sense of the implications for church life of what is done in liturgy. It is no surprise that in the postconciliar church there is often a clash between the rationality of hierarchical systems and the rationality of freedom and revolutionary ethic, espoused by some who see worship as superfluous, the only necessity being to follow the ethical mandate of Jesus Christ and thus change the world. One side identifies God's presence with a system, the other with ethical behavior. Neither side has a very subtle view of reality or of God's holiness, failing to perceive that the exigencies of the transcendent can be identified with no particular created reality or action. Faith is a force which remains a hope and a quest, a critical force challenging propensities to cry "peace, peace," or "behold the Lord."

When liturgical change and the introduction of the vernacular did not increase numerical participation in worship, when indeed it proved hard to accept, some bishops recognized that secularism was not simply a deviation tempting humanity to material values. They saw that it had to do with a basic vision of reality that comes out of modern experience, and that this vision clashed with much of what was taken for granted in liturgical rites, even when revised. There were several attempts to analyze this situation which veered away from a simple condemnation of the secular mentality, weighing both the positive and the negative and looking at the consequences for sacrament and evangelization. Indeed, one of the most significant steps was to link the issue of liturgical reform with that of evangelization.[14]

Three important factors emerged: (1) there cannot be liturgy without faith community, and this requires verification of both the human and the evangelical dimensions of common life; (2) faith in Jesus Christ requires a conversion, which is not identical to the acceptance of beliefs and teachings, nor even with changed patterns of moral life, but which is a change of heart, a way of looking at life and the transcendent, with repercussions on how one relates to the world, to society, to politics, and to all the issues that affect human potential and creativity; (3) some legitimate and necessary elements in a contemporary world view, and in a contemporary vision of the human person, are not allowed for adequately in the way that Christian teaching is proposed and that sacraments are celebrated.

As these perceptions were later developed and applied to liturgical renewal, people became more sensitive to issues of culture and to the pluralism of religious expression that steers away from uniformity and perfect unity. Others resist such issues, however, and it is not clear how far authority is willing to accept pluriformity in liturgy in those churches that remain dependent on the Western patriarchate of Rome. In fairness, it must be admitted that the reluctance to accept diversity is due not only to a desire for uniformity and concern over orthodoxy, but can also be occasioned or provoked by the tendency of some to adopt a new nonmedieval sacralism, to identify other cultural forms with the expression of the sacred. However, it is becoming clearer that the movement to greater cultural diversity in celebration is often linked with the challenge to become the church of the poor, a church which carries the promise of liberation in its preaching and in its liturgy.

SHORTCOMINGS OF THE HIERARCHICAL SYSTEM
Quite a profusion of studies attempt to analyze the cultural and religious crisis of the contemporary world, especially the Western world, and they all have implications for liturgy and its symbols. A common foundation of these studies is the principle that individuals and societies relate to the world and among themselves through symbol systems and myths, which represent reality in a nonrational way, in images and stories which evoke feelings and command relationships, and which promise well-being to those who adhere to the vision which they embody. For all the technological advance, intellectual sophistication, and organizational skill of the Western world, the coherence of life still requires symbolic expression. Values and possibilities are accepted only if persuasively presented to feelings. Consumerism is built upon this truth, and even rational systems which pretend to sophistication can succeed only if they carry within themselves their own mythologies. The response to the seductions of advertising and to the slickness of politicians and political parties is not to look for an honest world where symbolic appeal is unnecessary, but rather to bring people to greater individual freedom

and self-awareness where they can weigh their own reactions and differentiate between myths. While emotional appeal to a herd instinct is most decried in commercialism and politics, the confession has to be wrought that religious bodies have often behaved in a similar vein in pursuing their own ends. A symbolic system which confines and minimizes individual freedom and thought is no more acceptable in religion than in other fields.

The suppression of freedom and creativity in the liturgical history of the Roman Catholic Church, increasing demand for uniformity, the development of a clerically dominated institution, a concern for the poor which despite its good will failed to come to terms with social issues, are all matters which strike us today when we look into the past. Writers point to the kind of sacralism[15] which this represents, the seeds of which were sown quite early in church history. A diagnostic of the current situation in liturgical renewal and celebration postulates that the identification of God's truth and presence with a hierarchical system of priesthood and teaching be acknowledged and criticized.

It is possible to distinguish between the system and its abuses, however, and to recognize that the hierarchical system as such does not have to postulate identification between God and the ecclesial-social institution, between God's kingdom and the church, or between the kingdom and Christendom. Indeed, the better elements within the church have always recognized this nonidentity, without necessarily challenging the system's right to exist or questioning its divine origin. Great theologians such as Bonaventure and Thomas Aquinas recognized this nonidentity—in their pursuit of the way of negation and in propositions such as those which held that God's grace is not bound to the sacraments, or that the regulation of the moral life requires the principle of equity—precisely because no system or positive law can possibly cover all situations. In practice, the church has not been wanting for prophets who challenged abuses and preached the transcendence of God to the church, even while giving unremitting obedience to the hierarchy.

Therefore, clearing away abuses, recognizing the priority of the Word over the priesthood, living by the primacy of love rather than of obedience, recognizing gifts of the Spirit that complement those of the ordained ministry, allowing for greater lay participation and for more democratic ways in church life and in the practice of liturgy, all of this does not come to the heart of the matter or to the tensions intrinsic to the symbol system of which the liturgy is the primary conveyor, or indeed constituent. Rather, the heart of the matter is a fundamental view of the world and of God's relation to it.

The fascination with Francis of Assisi, wrought from history as contemporary hero, is telltale. We point to his prophetic role, to his challenge to wealth and hierarchical power in the church of his time, to his practice of evangelical poverty, and to his identification with the poor. Historical study reveals how much he was part of a movement or trend that was populist, interested in evangelical values and community, concerned about economic change and its social consequence, and above all conscious of the gospel imperative of love for the poor.[16] Respect for fact, however, makes us recognize his unswerving awe and respect for the priesthood and his unwavering obedience to the hierarchy, and above all to the papacy. Some appeal to Francis's obedience to argue in favor of church authority and to show that obedience to it is one of the qualities of holiness. The risk in this appeal is that it invites us to be uncritical about authority and the priesthood. Others react by saying that the mendicant movement, and Francis himself, fell victim to ecclesiastical and papal imperialism. This affected liturgy as well as other areas of life so that the Roman liturgy took on too much weight, and the popular forms of piety that went with the evangelical poverty movement were left peripheral to liturgy.

If we are to understand ourselves better in this Franciscan mirror, it needs to be underlined that Francis could hardly be anything else than tributary to a hierarchical system, given the mentality of the age to which he belonged. Whatever our admiration for his poverty and prophetic qualities, we are at odds with his overall vision of the world and of the church. Similarly, looking back to someone like Thomas Aquinas we learn how important it is to link theological method with subjective awareness, but we also realize that we do not operate out of the same sense of reality. Consequently, our ecclesial constructs and our liturgical devotion cannot be in easy harmony with his. Even though Aristotelian influence brought more interest in the created order and allowed for greater analysis of forms and essences than did neo-Platonism, with its view of all things as images of the divine, medieval theology viewed the world as determined by uniform metaphysical laws and principles and reasoned about the mysteries of faith accordingly. In church order, liturgy, and sacrament, the neo-Platonism of the Pseudo-Dionysius held sway, according to which the significance of ranked ministries and their priestly action lay in the fact that they were earthly manifestations of divine realities. The purpose of ecclesiastical power was thought to be to allow for a progressive divinization of the person, through assimilation, participation, and union with God. In face of this divine and ecclesiastical action, the laity remained passive and receptive, and though Aquinas demanded of all Christians an active profession of faith, and linked this with the sacrament of confirmation, he could only define the sacramental character of the baptized in terms of passive power. His analysis of human psychology and action, and his knowledge of Aristotelian categories, had allowed him to relate liturgical meaning and participation to intention, but when it was necessary to place this within a total systemic view he fell back on a hierarchical one.

The empirical sciences have brought to light that the world does not operate according to uniform metaphysical and physical laws, and that it is not possible to arrive at certitude by deduction from fixed first principles. One must attend much more to data, to the intelligibility of historical events in themselves, to change and flux in the material world and in the human world. Revelation itself may not be presented as doctrines and principles, but as God's presence in history. Meaning is discernible in the facts of history, in all its ebb and flow. The notion of science is one of investigation, experiment, and hypothesis. As this applies to natural sciences, so also it applies to study of the human world and of history, and this needs to be incorporated into our understanding of revelation and redemption. Faith and Christian belief cannot be identical with any fixed system of thought or institution. Their expression must allow for change and historical development, remaining open to the particular rather than being bound to universal categories. The word of revelation, the institutions of church life, the sacraments of worship, the teaching of the magisterium, the holy life, cannot be seen as representative images of divine truth and goodness. Indeed, the supposition we work with is one of nonidentity between them and the truth. They are given to us and need to develop as forms of quest and listening, as ways of relating to a transcendent truth in humility and aspiration, modes of God's presence in history which lead humanity in the way of eschatological hope. Moreover, it is not possible to keep a clear distinction between the sacred and the secular, in the sense that the holy is found in the church and intrudes on the secular only through the direct influence on it of church teaching and grace. In this new vision, the world itself, and its history, is the place where God is revealed and experienced, and it is out of life lived in love and service that one approaches the mysteries of creation, redemption, and God.

The symbolic expression that corresponds to this kind of vision is more historical than figurative, more communal than hierarchical. Rather than presenting its participants with images of universal divine truth, liturgy can offer some disclosure of the various ways in which Jesus Christ and the Spirit are present among the people and in the flux of historical events. Proclamation of the word and celebration of the sacraments as actions of a believing community become ways whereby it begins to relate to history, the eschatological nature of which is accepted on God's promise.

A further problem with a traditional hierarchical or sacral model of the Christian symbol system is that such a model remains relatively undifferentiated in its appeal and influence. It appeals to the psyche and to faith in a way that makes little distinction between common sense, theory, affectivity, and responsible decision. Indeed, its appeal is more affective than anything else, and what it asks is a surrender to God through obedience to the word or to the priesthood, and through awe of the actions of the ordained minister. A knowledge of mysteries and right conduct

are presumed to flow from this reverence and
obedience. A distinction between the intellectual and
the affective is not adverted to, except when it is seen
as an aberration. The need for responsible reflection in
order to arrive at ethical decisions seems unnecessary,
because conduct is dictated by the clear norms of
priestly teaching.

DIFFERENTIATION OF CONSCIOUSNESS

A large part of the problem in liturgical renewal is that
we hear and use liturgical language in a frame of mind
that does not fit well with its way of speech and
signifying. One of the principles laid down by Vatican
II for the reform of rites was that language should be
simple and intelligible. The effort to implement this in
translating texts into the vernacular and in modifying
symbols has often resulted in banality. The attempt was
to offer texts and rites that were either technically or
descriptively clear, whereas the language of liturgy fits
into the genus of the poetic. The confusion between
these kinds of speech belabors the liturgical renewal.
The answer to the difficulty is not to ignore the
distinction but to be more clearly conscious of it, as this
is now possible in ways not available to previous
generations.

In his recent book on the Bible and literature, *The Great
Code,* Northrop Frye remarks on how Western
civilization has passed through three great stages in the
use of language and in ways of thinking about reality.[17]
He calls these the mythological, the metonymic, and
the descriptive. When society became more
sophisticated, it learned how to distinguish among
these modes, but in its passion for new discoveries, it
also tended to lose the contribution to wholeness of
earlier stages. This is to its detriment, because each
stage represents aspects of reality and of humanity's

part in total reality that need to be integrated into life. One might say that living with such differentiation presents a difficulty and a challenge, but when culture has taught us how to differentiate we cannot ignore its necessity.

The Mythological Stage

The mythological stage of thought and speech, according to Frye, is one where people expressed their sense of reality and their part in it through stories, symbols, and rituals. They made no clear distinctions between truth and fiction, subject and object, humanity and nature, or between the transcendent and the earthly. All reality was presented in a unified way, and nature was envisaged as being endowed with divine energies. Language allowed human persons to participate in this reality, or was even viewed as a force which affected the course of reality since it had its own power.

The Metonymic Stage

In the metonymic stage of thought and language, a distinction was made between reality and thought, between words and thought, and so also between different kinds of language. Things could be spoken of not only mythologically but also theoretically, so that mythological language was dubbed metaphorical. Nature could be spoken of as though it were inhabited by divinities, but theory taught the difference between the two orders, between the transcendent and the earthly, as it also taught the difference between the appearance of things and their essential reality. A human person and an animal may look very much alike, and mythology confuses the two, but theory teaches the distinction in what it says of the rational mind and the soul.

The Descriptive Stage

The third stage of language and thought is the empirical or descriptive. This is linked with the advance of positive sciences. In this third stage, not only mythology but also theory is discarded. Persons and societies put confidence only in what is empirically verifiable and liable to be scrutinized in some positive way. The world of mythology is deemed unsophisticated and the world of speculative thought unreal. Therefore, the challenge to our age is to hold the three modes together, not by ignoring the differences but by respecting them.

Liturgy and its interpretation must take account of this differentiated mode of speech. It is not possible to subscribe to a naive view of worship that confuses appearances with reality. To take account of the distinction between the mythological and the theoretical, it is possible to take account of the difference between images and what they represent.[18] Keeping the language of myth and metaphor in liturgy does not mean that it is the projection of a fanciful world by persons unaware of the difference between myth and theory. On the contrary, upholding the need for the imaginative in an age that pursues verifiable knowledge and fact is an acknowledgment of the limits of science. The imaginative expresses the existence of a world that is not subject to empirical investigation. Furthermore, the language of the imagination appeals to the affective as well as to the cognitional. The distinction between the cognitional and the affective points to the psychic roots of human dwelling in the world and to the need to keep in touch with these roots, however clear-sighted we may think our vision is.[19] We learn from them as they are explicitated in symbolic expression. Their explicitation contributes to a conversion of heart that is purifying and humble, because it is that of a heart ready to encounter the darkness as well as the light. Symbolic usage that lays claim to clarity and ignores deep-seated roots in nature and affinities with the unconscious becomes a veiled claim to false rationality. The aesthetic side of a symbol system is more clearly seen because of this advertence to the affective. The value of symbols in transforming experience is better appreciated, while at the same time it is not confused with the appeal to emotion that quietens questions and probing into the roots of behavior.

This perception of the contemporary mind and world view is comparable with Paul Ricoeur's conviction that today we cannot inhabit the language of symbol without understanding it. His program of demythologization and demystification lays the groundwork for the retrieval of such language.[20] Demythologization breaks the connection between what is said and what is meant. This leaves open a space for one to grasp that what is intended is not the mere facticity of a story or of an image, but the mode of human dwelling that is disclosed in the story and the power of grace which transforms it. Gone is the time when it was possible to accept the story of Adam and Eve as a recounting of what happened at the beginning of the world. Yet, this does not mean that the story is without significance for us. It can be heard, through interpretation, as a universal story which speaks to any generation about the conditions of finitude and sin under which humanity labors, about the tensions of evil present in history, and about the promises of salvation that go with faith and trust in God. Gone too is the possibility of seeing baptism as a cleansing from inherited sin, but this does not mean that the images of stain, inheritance, and regeneration are without significance. Their significance can be captured if we refer them to the communal, personal, and historical experience of being born in a world of sinfulness and of the impossibility of being saved without divine graciousness. In short, demythologization alerts us to the cultural vehicle in which the kerygma is presented and the faith celebrated. By keeping a distance from this cultural vehicle, the meaning for all ages can be expressed in terms appropriate to a new cultural experience.

DOMINATION AND DEMYSTIFICATION

The program of demystification is necessary[21] because symbols express and effect the distribution of power (personal, social, creative, organizational, traditional, transformative). The deployment of such power has been too closely identified with ecclesiastical, social, and political systems, which block its more general communication and sharing. Religious practice and religious institutions harbor and foster many illusions which mask the meaning of the original event, give rise to false consciousness, and prevent people from fully hearing the word of Christ or from receiving the inner power of the Spirit. One has to be suspicious of the ways in which the Christian symbol system has evolved or liturgy is celebrated.[22] To the contemporary masters of suspicion[23] one has to concede the unconscious and hidden influence of sexual, economic, and political factors on church life and sacramental celebration, and the domination of the weak by the strong. Uncovering these influences is a way of retrieving the original power of the symbols, of positing the nonidentity between system and symbol, between God and ritual or institution, and of overcoming the atrophy of communication within church and liturgy which paralyzes liturgical celebration, and as a result paralyzes the missionary life of the church in the world.

In effect, the false mysticism surrounding rites and institutions means that authority and sacrament became means of instrumental action. Such action tries to produce results and make things work, rather than serve creative forces among the people and make a more broadly based contribution to the common good. Some analyses of the dominance in Western society of instrumental thinking and action find that its prevalence in the secular stems ultimately from the religious systems of earlier centuries, of which the enlightenment and the empirical sciences constituted a critique.[24] At first, empirical sciences such as psychology and sociology questioned the universality and uniformity which authority systems upheld, contributing even to certain kinds of power in the political world. Yet in time, the empirical sciences themselves fell prey to bureaucracy and social manipulation. As Matthew Lamb puts it, the illusion of a god identical with the ecclesiastical system has been replaced by one of a humanity identical with certain political and economic systems, and the empirical sciences all too often feed into this illusion.[25]

Political theologians and liberation theologies remind us that systems—whether political, economic, or religious—have victims whose rights and place in society are denied and suppressed, whose lives are less free and creative because they are dominated by those in power. They are the poor who are subject to the authority of those in control or those who interpret. They cannot act freely as agents of their own history, let alone find the conditions for a full human life. They are the cultural, religious, social, and ethnic minorities, who must find their place in relation to the majority, who are not free to think out their own future in terms of their own heritage and creative forces. They are women, who politics classifies as wives and daughters and religion as Eve. Sacramental practice itself is treated with suspicion by theologians of liberation, because it often shares in the control which leads to victimization.[26]

In the face of such observations, two things affecting liturgical development can be mentioned. One is the attention given in worship to memory, the other the attention given in current thought to popular religion or religiosity. Of course memory is at the heart of liturgy, but political theology points out that freedom can be won by remembering the victims, as well as those who have lived lives of solidarity with the victims, and by remembering what history suppresses in a kind of massive forgetfulness.[27] Into the memory of Jesus Christ the church can gather all those who have in the course of history been victimized by systems and by the hatreds which they engender, as well as all those who in freedom of spirit have resisted victimization.

The study of popular religiosity is often without clear focus and risks becoming a mere fashion. It is certainly not an unambiguous phenomenon. It can be fostered by a system of government as one mode of keeping control of the people. On the part of those who practice it, it can represent a way of acquiescing in their state, of dealing with it without resisting the prevailing system. It can also be a sign of protest, a keeping alive of alternative models of community and religion, an expression of the poor which contrasts with that of the powerful, a residue of forces which prevents the dominant in society or church from having the future all to themselves.[28]

The model of community presented in popular religion—one of cultivating bonds among people and with nature, of acknowledging God and the sacred in the midst of daily life—tends to be forced out in contemporary society. Its elimination can have dire consequences. Some history is laudatory of ecclesiastical authorities for the way they have always tolerated, or even fostered, popular religion alongside liturgy. Whatever can be said about praise or blame, popular religion represents a way of relating to cosmos and bios, and of developing human relations, which is fast disappearing. This disappearance contributes to a crisis of culture and spirituality. Its persistence reminds us that it is not enough to demythologize and demystify. It is also necessary to keep symbolic language alive, to incorporate the symbolism of popular culture, but in incorporating it to learn how to interpret it. Demythologization and demystification uncover illusions, but risk leaving a void or an excessive confidence in the human subject's capacity to shape both reality and self. Uncovering illusions invites a deeper interpretation and a creative development of the symbolic. The illusions are themselves a reminder that we do not have immediate access either to reality or to self-consciousness. This is always mediated through image and language. To ignore this and to replace the myths that are abandoned with a sense of power and the use of technology is to contribute to a crisis of human dwelling.

MODEL OF SYMBOLIC RETRIEVAL
Gibson Winter has investigated recently the loss of the symbolic in Western life and terms it a crisis in spirituality.[29] He talks of this crisis as a clash between two mentalities and systems of common or social life. One of these he calls mechanistic and the other organicist. He sees them as two different paradigms for understanding and shaping human life and humanity's part in the life of the world. Although each of the systems can be identified in large part with particular bodies of persons, at a deeper level they are at war with each other in the whole cultural and social fabric of Western society, awaiting a resolution that can reconcile them.

The mechanistic paradigm is one of a development of particular and global society on the basis of an expansion of human powers of control and exploitation. It offers free rein to analytic science and technological organization, and in the process does much to offer solutions to human problems of hunger and disease, as well as providing opportunities for more affluent living. It exalts the autonomy and freedom of the individual, and suggests that this is the basis for a better future. The organicist paradigm, on the other hand, locates real power in the integrity of peoples and communities and looks to the models of human and social relations, and to what the paradigm projects as the common good, before it looks to the autonomy or creative powers of the individual. Bonds among peoples, bonds with nature, a sense of the sacred in the cosmos and in life, have priority over technical organization and scientific development.

Winter affirms that it is the prevalence of the mechanistic paradigm in public life, and the practical suppression of the organicist, which causes the crisis of Western spirituality. This crisis threatens the very existence of the human race. Of course, he does not suggest a simple return to the organicist paradigm, since it seems unable to incorporate the genuine possibilities of progress, but he does believe that many of its virtues need to be kept alive and given their place in projections of the future. Practical projections of the future cannot be made, however, without an adequate symbolic projection. This projection must be effected by a retrieval of our symbolic heritage that responds to the two mentalities and resolves their conflict in a more encompassing vision than either of them is able to project alone.

For Winter, the key elements of such a symbolic projection will be a sense of history and a paradigm of artistic creation. He favors the paradigm of artistic creation, because he believes that the artist is sensitive to humanity's relation to cosmos and bios, possesses a sense of reverence for the holy and the transcendent, and is stimulated by those insights from cultural heritage which allow for a transformative renewal of the present. Artists do not simply reproduce the past, nor do they merely depict external impressions and experiences. Winter hopes for a sensibility to the powers that humanity now knows it possesses, accompanied by sensibility to the values of the past. Without this double sensibility the future cannot be creatively projected.

To a liturgist who believes that sacrament is of its nature attuned to the creative process of bios and cosmos, that the sacramental heritage talks of ways of communion among peoples, with nature, and with the God who is revealed in Jesus Christ, that a sense of history is its eschatological core, and that the Christian community is richly endowed with the imagination that, in tune with the Spirit, can draw on this heritage to transform experience, this is a challenging analysis of the contemporary human condition.

CONCLUSION

Without rushing too hastily into a definition of symbol, or into a description of how symbols work, and taking it for granted that the sacramental is a symbolic system, this chapter has presented the challenge to this symbolic system that the church must meet in reforming and renewing the liturgy. The liturgical renewal is not a simple matter of reviving what history tells us are more authentic rites, nor of working out of a better grasp of the meaning of core symbols. The Christian communities must meet the challenge of relating contemporary experience to a symbolic heritage, transforming that experience in the power of

30

the Spirit, and projecting the kind of future for humanity that is promised in the symbol of God's kingdom and in the memory of Jesus Christ.

From an initial advertence to the crisis, it was possible to highlight the crisis of the hierarchical world view that is embodied in our liturgical past, as well as to describe the conscious awareness available to us of the complexity of the human spirit. From Paul Ricoeur, the suggestion was taken that demythologization and demystification are necessary parts of the program of symbolic retrieval, and the applicability of this to liturgical renewal was indicated. Political and liberation theologies were mentioned as indicators of the need to keep the memory of victims in a liberating liturgy. Popular religion was invoked as a reminder, not only of victims, but also of past ways of relating to nature, of living in human community, and of embracing God, that cannot be wholly deserted even in this more sophisticated technological age. Finally, Gibson Winter provided the elements of historical consciousness and artistic paradigm as keys to a liturgical renewal of symbolic heritage. Paradoxically, this paradigm is a reminder that liturgical change cannot be programmed according to the postulates of the hierarchical system in question. Christian intuition, concern for freedom, joy of celebration, and the gifts of the aesthetic that reside not in priests and scholars but among the people will be the authentic agents of liturgical renewal. This is not to suggest that there will be no bishops or ordained ministers in the church of the future. It is only to recall that in the past, too much of the understanding of church and sacrament was tied up with the operations of the ordained, both speculatively and practically, because that view harmonized with a vision of an ordered universe. In the future, the functioning of the symbol system needs to have a broader ecclesial basis and to represent a more historical perspective on world and kingdom.

NOTES

1. Susanne K. Langer, *Philosophy in a New Key: A Study in the Symbolism of Reason, Rite, and Art,* 3rd ed. (Cambridge, Mass.: Harvard University Press, 1978), p. 289.

2. Ibid., p. 288.

3. Ibid., p. 289.

4. Joseph Campbell, *Creative Mythology, The Masks of God,* vol. 4 of *Creative Mythology* (New York: Viking Press, 1968).

5. James Joyce, *A Portrait of the Artist as a Young Man* (New York: Penguin, 1964), p. 253.

6. See the lines from W. B. Yeats's poem "The Second Coming":
   Things fall apart; the centre cannot hold;
   Mere anarchy is loosed upon the world.

7. Nathan A. Scott, "The broken center: a definition of the crisis of values in modern literature," in Rollo May (ed.), *Symbolism in Religion and Literature* (New York: Braziller, 1960), pp. 178–202.

8. Terence Brown, *Ireland: A Social and Cultural History 1922–79* (Glasgow: Fontana Paperbacks, 1981).

9. Ibid., p. 325.

10. On the meaning of ideology in this context see Clifford Geertz, "Ideology as a cultural system," in *The Interpretation of Cultures* (New York: Basic Books, 1973), pp. 193–233. The word is also used pejoratively, to indicate how systems are dominated by false consciousness.

11. Several of the essays in *The Interpretation of Cultures,* especially "Ethos, World View, and the Analysis of Sacred Symbols," pp. 126–141.

12. Geertz, "Ideology," p. 218.

13. J.-P. Jossua, "La Constitution 'Sacrosanctum Concilium' dans l'ensemble de l'oeuvre conciliaire," in Y. Congar & J.-P. Jossua (eds.), *La Liturgie après Vatican II* (Paris: Cerf, 1967), pp. 127–58.

14. See for example the report of the French episcopacy *Lourdes 1971: L'Eglise Signe de Salut au Milieu des Hommes* (Paris: Centurion, 1972).

15. Matthew Lamb, *Solidarity with Victims: Towards a Theology of Social Transformation* (New York: Crossroad, 1982), pp. 17–19, 35.

16. Lester K. Little, *Religious Poverty and the Profit Economy in Medieval Europe* (Ithaca, N.Y.: Cornell University Press, 1978); and M. Mollat, "The poverty of Francis: A Christian and social option," in *Concilium* 149 (Edinburgh: Clark, 1981), pp. 23–29.

17. Northrop Frye, *The Great Code: The Bible and Literature* (New York & London: Harcourt Brace Jovanovich, 1982), pp. 3–30.

18. On differentiation see Bernard Lonergan, *Method in Theology* (New York: Herder & Herder, 1972), pp. 256–66.

19. Robert Doran, "Psychic conversion," *The Thomist* 41 (1977), 200–36; "Aesthetic subjectivity and generalized empirical method," *The Thomist* 43 (1979), 257–78.

20. Among his works, see for example "The critique of religion," in Charles E. Reagan & David Stewart (eds.), *The Philosophy of Paul Ricoeur: An Anthology of His Work* (Boston: Beacon Press, 1978), pp. 213–22.

21. Ricoeur, in Reagan & Stewart.

22. This point will be developed later in the book.

23. The name given by Ricoeur to Freud, Marx, and Nietzsche.

24. Lamb, pp. 34–36.

25. Ibid., pp. 52, 123–125.

26. See for example Juan Luis Segundo, *Sacraments Today* (Maryknoll, N.Y.: Orbis, 1973). On how this relates to the women's issue see Mary Collins, "The public language of ministry," *The Jurist* 41:2 (1981), 261–294.

27. On memory see J. B. Metz, *Faith in History and Society: Toward a Practical Fundamental Theology* (New York: Seabury Press, 1980), pp. 184–204.

28. André Aubry, "The feast of peoples and the explosion of society—popular practice and liturgical practice," *Concilium* 142 (Edinburgh: Clark, 1981), pp. 55–64.

29. Gibson Winter, *Liberating Creation: Foundations of Religious Social Ethics* (New York: Crossroad, 1981), pp. 97–111.

Chapter Two

Historical Interlude

In a reflection on the relation between Christian symbol and contemporary culture, it is useful to note different ways in which symbols have been used, interpreted, and appropriated in the course of church history. The survey offered here is not exhaustive. Rather, it indicates factors from history that are pertinent to present need and that help to better understand liturgy's symbolic nature, because present issues have roots in history.

THE NEW TESTAMENT PERIOD[1]

Christian worship grew out of practices already in vogue. As early Christians professed their faith in Jesus Christ and in remembering him continued to worship God in familiar forms, they found many elements in their communal prayer life challenged and modified. There was the need to set aside what was inconsistent with belief in Jesus Christ, to relate everything to the commemoration of his deeds and words, and to assimilate new elements that were required by the centrality of the new faith. The historical account of how Christian worship developed from its Jewish matrix must reckon with what was assimilated from this matrix, how Christian worship modified it, what was discarded, and what new elements were appropriated from other sources as Christian communities were born in the diaspora.[2]

The principal point is how worship gradually centered around the symbolism of the cross, or obtained its specific character from the remembrance of the cross. This was by no means a straightforward process, since early Christian communities had not worked out all the implications of belief in Jesus Christ, nor all that was implied in the hope that the promised salvation had come in him. Belief in Jesus' lordship did not at once involve the soteriological significance of the cross. As questions of soteriology developed, however, the cross and its remembrance became the determining factor in ritual and in symbolic development. This is not the place to resolve the intricate questions surrounding the origins of the Lord's Supper and the emergence of the Christian anaphora from Jewish blessings or *berakoth*. Suffice to say that both ritual and prayer developed in a way that highlighted the cross as central to Christian remembrance. Similarly, many of the issues about the ritual which Christians adopted for baptism are not finally resolved, but again its specific characteristic became the act of faith in the cross of Christ and the incorporation into his death.[3]

The second point is that belief in the cross included resurrection symbolism and belief. Indeed, belief in the Risen Lord and the expectation of his return preceded a clear soteriological understanding of his death.[4]

The significance of belief in the death and resurrection of Jesus is expressed in historical narrative. Symbolic expression transforms experience by expressing new meaning. Historical symbols are a way of connecting historical events and interpreting historical flow. The gospels constantly interpret the death and works of Jesus through the symbols of the Old Testament and Judaism. It is enough here to take one event that is central to Christian worship, the words over the cup in the accounts of the Last Supper. Peculiar to these words is how they weave together a remembrance of the covenant, the Passover, the preaching of Jeremiah on the new covenant, and the figure of the servant of Yahweh in the Deutero-Isaiah. It is by this collective and historical memory that the death of Jesus is interpreted and is itself in turn remembered.[5]

The remembrance of Jesus Christ and of his death meant a desacralization of worship in Christian communities, one that took place progressively rather than all at once. This means that certain sacral practices important to Judaism were discontinued without specific replacement. Good examples are temple worship, circumcision, and Sabbath observance. As Christians began to look more like a sect, they were unwelcome in the temple and synagogues, which led them to ask whether such practices were necessary. At the same time, they apparently felt some inconsistencies between these practices and belief in Christ. Diaspora communities were naturally less attached to them than inhabitants of Judea, and the incorporation of Gentiles into the church had its repercussions on views about the Jewish people and their place in salvation history. These practices were interpreted as types that were given their fulfillment in Jesus Christ and in the church as antitypes. Their disappearance signaled a change in the way that roles and relations in a covenant community were viewed, especially that Christians had no priesthood and no sacrifice other than the remembrance of Jesus, their obedience to the gospel, and their praise of God. The very notion of worship itself developed around these realities rather than around cult and priesthood.

To desacralize is not the same thing as to discard, of course, but rather to assimilate the images attached to sacred ritual and the significance of ritual into a nonritualistic context, thus changing the meaning of the holy. The New Testament calls no member of the community "priest" and has no place for priestly ritual, but it retains priestly imagery in its designation of the people saved in Jesus Christ and of their actions done in obedience to the gospel. The transforming power of the Spirit is expressed in the lively images taken from accounts of God's presence in the temple. Since this transformation comes through belief in Jesus Christ, and since obedience to the gospel became central to the notion of worship in the community, charisms of word took on a central place not only in building up the people but in the new imagery of worship. Those gifted with these charisms were not given any place of privilege or sacral distinction, but they did command authority precisely because of the importance of word. The new interaction between life and community celebration parallels this appreciation for gifts of word. Acts of community prayer gave pride of place to hearing the word, to narrative commemoration, and to thanks and praise, rather than to priestly acts.

The view of reality expressed in this movement follows a historical and eschatological model rather than a cosmological one. God is celebrated in the remembrance of history, not in wonder at the hierophanies of nature. What Christians retained from Jewish liturgy was its historical remembrance rather than its priestly activity. Furthermore, the eschatological expectation of Judaism received a new turn by reason of the belief that the awaited kingdom had come in Jesus Christ.

This move away from temple and priesthood to people, word, and deed is sometimes called the *spiritualization* of worship and sacrifice.[6] It is not to be thought that spiritualization occurred only in Christianity at that time. Historians of religion in late antiquity remark that civilization in general in the first Christian centuries was marked by an anthropological turn, over against a cosmological vision of reality.[7] That is, civilization placed the center of world meaning in humanity and in the doings of human societies, not in humanity's conformity to cosmic patterns. Historians of Judaism in turn point to a historical, asacral, and acosmological element in Jewish worship right from its origins, and to the turn toward greater spiritualization which it took in the diaspora after the destruction of Jerusalem and the dispersion of the Jews.[8]

It is useful to note this, not to reduce Christian worship to a kind of common cultural phenomenon, but to show how in its own development it dealt with a tension that seems native to the religious instinct and that continues to make its presence felt in the historical evolution of Christian forms of worship. This comparison with a more general understanding of religious movements leaves intact the fact that Christian developments centered around the historical memory of Jesus and the cross.

Since to worship is to remember Jesus Christ and God's work in him, the Jewish practice of memorial became central to Christian observance.[9] This is evident in the Lord's Supper by reason of the ordinance "do this as a memorial of me," but the description can be applied to all prayers and rites. A key idea in Jewish cult was that acts of worship were done in memory of past salvific events, so that the people could continue to participate in them and receive the promises of God that they contained. This sense of memorial is to the fore in the Last Supper narratives in the gospels and in Paul. John and Luke, however, add a note of personal memory.[10] Jesus asks that his disciples remember him as a servant. This is the testament that he leaves to them and that is recalled in worship as well as in word. Christians remember not only a historical act in which God acted for their salvation, but they also remember a person. The more abstract quality of historical deliverance, where an action in narration is given abstract form, is counterbalanced by the remembrance of the one whose chief earthly characteristic was to act as a servant to those whom he was not ashamed to call brothers and sisters.

In brief, the points about symbol that have been drawn from the New Testament are the following. Primary is the centrality of the cross of the one who was put to death and raised up. Second, there are the historical and eschatological meanings of Christian symbolism that occur in keeping memory. Third, there is the desacralization that goes with the turn to person and community, and what this implies about the relation between liturgy and moral practice.

THE PATRISTIC ERA

In turning to the patristic era, one can distinguish between practices and the way in which symbolism was understood. As for practices, it is important to note the realities of cultural adaptation, mystagogical catechesis, the effects on worship of the adoption of an initiation schema during a period of church expansion, and elements of resacralization, especially in the understanding and exercise of ministry.

Cultural Adaptation

In introducing the Second Vatican Council, Pope John XXIII raised the issue of preaching the gospel to a contemporary culture, and made a distinction between its substance and the cultural modes wherein it is interpreted and preached. This distinction was then applied to liturgy, where the avowed policy was to distinguish the central rites from the rest. This done, these former could be given the prominence they demand, leaving room in further revisions for cultural differences which would not affect the substance. The principle had some appeal and served the functional purpose of simplifying rites, but its usefulness is probably past.

In their research into the history of liturgy, scholars have tried to get behind cultural differences to some basic schema of worship. As studies progress, this becomes more and more difficult, since at any stage of development, even the earliest, one finds differences and the need to take account of a variety of cultural influences. A good example of this is the investigation of the origins of the eucharist, and more particularly of the eucharistic prayer. As a result of many careful studies done by scholars of different Christian traditions, recent ecumenical statements have outlined a schema for the great prayer of thanksgiving, one that settles its general form but leaves room for differences.[11] Even as such statements are issued, however, it becomes apparent that the schema does not take all of the facts of liturgical history into account, and that it might be more rigid than is necessary.[12]

Historical studies must take account of Semitic and Hellenic influences on Christian worship. The question arises whether Christianity, being a historical religion, must necessarily retain some features of Semitic and Hellenic cultures. Or is it possible to translate everything that is essential to worship into new cultural modes? In our own time, this question is raised, for example, in non-Western countries, where an attempt is made to adopt the idiom of Asian or African cultures at such vital moments as the eucharistic prayer.[13] The same question is raised in the West when, for example, it is asked whether the address to God as "Abba" may not, as far as meaning is concerned, allow for the adoption of very different names.[14]

These hermeneutical questions are too large to answer here, but it is sufficient to note the constant cultural adaptation of liturgy during the first millenium of church history and the cultural diversity of early centuries. This touches on space, ritual, language, ministry, customs for the burial of the dead, practices of penance, and other sundry matters. Among Jews in the diaspora, the model for gathering was the house and the common table. In a free Rome, the model for gathering was the basilica, and when Christians were recognized as an integral part of the Roman world they adopted this model for liturgy. Among northern peoples, the model for celebration was the shrine to the divinity, and Nordic Christians adopted this model. The real issue seems to be not the legitimacy of these models, but whether in adopting them the churches kept spiritual freedom or lost it in part or in whole. For example, did the model of the shrine bring back elements of cosmic religion, an inevitable link to sacred places and sacred times in a religion that was intended to be free of such bonds? Did the influence of the imperial court on Roman liturgy bring back into the community distinctions between persons that were supposed to have been overcome in Christ?

It is easy to note the cultural diversity in early worship, once the necessary studies are done. It is more difficult to find the criteria with which to assess the impact of cultural influences. At this stage it is only possible to anticipate the difference between the historical and the hierophanic which will be explored more fully in later chapters. In brief, of different cultural models in the early church one can ask whether they allow for the essential nature of Christian worship as a memorial of Jesus Christ and a proclamation of the word, or whether they subordinate this characteristic to manifestations of the holy in sacred places, times, and persons. This is not to discountenance the importance of the visual and the sensory in worship. It is only to ask how they are integrated into a worship that is essentially memorial.

Mystagogical Catechesis
By mystagogical catechesis is meant the teaching given to neophytes on sacraments after their baptism. It is

based on sacramental experience, prepared for by a catechumenate that engaged candidates in hearing the word, in learning to pray, and in moral development, but that contained no explicit reference to the sacraments whereby they were to enter the body of the church. Those who were ready in faith to commit themselves to Jesus Christ were admitted to the symbolic experience and then afterward invited to probe its meaning through a reflection on the symbols they had experienced. The principal examples that we have of early mystagogical catechesis are the instructions given to their churches by Cyril of Jerusalem, Ambrose of Milan, Theodore of Mopsuestia, and John Chrysostom.[15]

These bishops do not present a common, uniform explanation for each item of the sacramental liturgy. Indeed, the flexibility of their explanations is notable and is a reminder that it is unwise to reduce symbolic meaning to the conceptual or descriptive. They draw their explanations from three different sources: nature, culture, and the Bible, the last being the most important.

The principle on which this catechesis is based is that the sacraments are a participation in the mysteries of Christ, through representation and imitation. Therefore, the major content of the instructions is an explanation of how at the various moments of the celebration the participants are brought to share in the cross and resurrection and to take on a life that is changed by this sharing. Here as elsewhere in patristic writing, typology is one of the major instruments of interpretation. Christ and the church are seen to be prefigured in Old Testament events and symbols, just as the liturgy which recalls these figures anticipates eternal life and the resurrection of the flesh. To support this biblical input, the catechists draw on the natural symbolism of such elements as water, fire, darkness, light, nakedness, and body movement. They also include explanations drawn from the current cultural scene. Thus, the military oath serves as a similitude for the renunciation of Satan and the commitment to Jesus Christ.

Mystagogical catechesis is certainly not an isolated genre, but has much in common with patristic interpretation of the scriptures and homiletic material in general. It has been singled out here simply because it is a very concrete and accessible example of how the Fathers of the church interpreted the sacraments.

The Initiation Schema
Nowadays it is very common to speak of the sacraments of initiation and to adopt the metaphor of initiation to describe the spiritual life of the Christian. However, metaphors of enlightenment were more common in the earliest centuries and admittance into the church did not necessarily entail the long period of preparation that is associated with the history of the catechumenate.[16] The development of the catechumenate and of a period of penance for sinners was the church's response to the necessities of a Christianity that was given state recognition and that grew in numbers at least partly as a result of this recognition. In the circumstances under which Christian peoples lived, conversion was achieved through a process extending over a period of time, and hence the schema, if not the term, of initiation was adopted, both for entry into the church and for penitents. It was also adopted increasingly as an image to describe the entire spiritual life of Christians.

This schema emphasized what today is seen as process and development through a gradual assimilation of beliefs, customs, practices, and moral norms. It had an ascetical note to it and was prone to adopt images of commitment and purification, by way of contrast with

44

the celebration of enlightenment and transformation that marked the beginnings of the Christian faith. The initiation schema also affected the interpretation of the mystery of Christ, so that increasingly Christ's death was interpreted as a transition through death to the life of the resurrection rather than as a victory over death.

Such an approach to the practice and explanation of sacrament and liturgy is associated with what is now called the nourishing role of the church and of its pastoral ministry. When people were born into a Christian culture, where the sole accessible forms of religious practice were Christianity or what were considered deviations from it, the church accepted the responsibility of nourishing them in the faith from cradle to grave and of providing the appropriate religious ceremony for all occasions, those of family and those of public life. No longer were Christians groups of people going against the grain, committed to a faith of which they saw the transforming power and the promise. The effect of this transition on the practice and theory of liturgy has to be reckoned with in any contemporary renewal and acculturation of worship.

Resacralization
Along with the adoption of an initiation schema went a process of resacralization. That is to say, the desacralization of persons of rank, of places, and of time which marked New Testament Christianity was to some extent reversed in the making of a religion of popular appeal and practice. The pastoral role became increasingly one of guidance to those who needed exhortations to right practice and belief, and whose various religious wants had to be met by appropriate devotions and festivals. People needed to link their religious observance to the seasons of the year, and they yearned for vivid religious ceremonial. How could pastors wean them away from pagan observances unless they provided festival and sacrament for the

seasons of the calendar and of human life? Christmas and other feasts, such as that of John the Baptist on June 24, have some connection with prior pagan solemnities.[17] In evangelizing the peoples of northern Europe, apostles and pastors were well aware of the attraction of holy places, so they often replaced pagan temples with Christian sanctuaries.

In the course of such developments, a return to priestly and sacrificial nomenclature occurred, one that was given support by an appeal to imagery from the Old Testament writings. Christology took a turn which underlined the sacrificial atonement for sin which Christ made through his death on the cross, and this found echoes in the celebration of the eucharist, which increasingly highlighted images of sacrifice and priesthood. This turn also affected the lives of the ordained. In documents such as the papal decretals of the fourth and fifth centuries, the rule of clerical continence was supported by the use of texts and images which in the Old Testament spoke of the Levitical priesthood.[18]

Patristic Thought
Whatever their adaptations to pastoral need and cultural practice, the thought of the church Fathers retained a notion of the sacramental which is in strong contrast with later Western patterns. Terms such as symbol, mimesis, figure, and icon denote a presence of Christ's mysteries in sacrament, not merely a representation of them that inspires devotion and feeling, nor merely the effective grace that comes from them. Moreover, the sacramental covers a very broad field. In the homilies of St. Leo the Great, for example, sacrament includes the Christ-event, the reality of the church, the liturgical cycle, and the elements of each particular celebration, such as the proclamation of the gospel, the prayer of thanksgiving, and the ritual acts.[19]

From there, it extends to include the lives of the faithful which are lived out as an imitation of Christ's mysteries, an imitation grounded in the liturgical celebration. One might paraphrase patristic thought on the sacramental by saying that for the Fathers reality is one, of which there are many manifestations and participations, all of them interwined.

One of the major benefits of this way of thinking is that it keeps alive and vivid the unity of the mystery of redemption. Christ and the church are the new creation, in which God's love is present and manifest. Sacraments are not mysteries of Christ *and* the church, but mysteries of Christ *in* the church and of the church *in* Christ. Liturgy is not the sole symbolic reality, but it belongs alongside the scriptures and other manifestations such as icons. It is distinct from these not in being symbolic but in being the gathering and celebration of the body, the place where the church assumes its full form, bringing into a common expression of faith and joy all the other symbols that belong in the mystery.

The liturgy thus unites in one action: (1) the presence and action of Christ in the church through the Spirit (*epiclesis*); (2) the proclamation of Christ in the scriptures and the memorial (*anamnesis*) kept of him; (3) the feasts of the liturgical cycle which incorporate elements of historical and cosmic symbolism; (4) the use of material things, such as bread, wine, oil, and water, as well as of material actions, such as immersion, eating, drinking, and anointing, which become in the celebration the *typos, symbol,* or *eikon* of divine mysteries, by virtue of an assumption into the commemorative ritual of the natural and cultural significance which they already possess; (5) the action of faith, expressed in various modes of prayer, wherein the sealing of the Spirit illumines the mind to perceive God's truth.

Whatever admiration patristic thought arouses, one cannot ignore its neo-Platonic strain when it integrates the symbolic. It is built on the notion that lesser realities participate in the higher and eventually all things converge into one. Because of faith in Jesus Christ, the vision of reality is finally historical and allows a place for the material and for the various forms of representation which Greek philosophy does not entertain. Nonetheless, the strain creates a gap between patristic and contemporary thought. The contemporary mind wonders how seriously the Fathers took finite beings in their own distinctive reality and how seriously they took history, since they tended to see all events by way of reference to a divine and eternal design.

To understand the intricacies of symbolic interpretation and usage more fully, we can now take note of two very different types of neo-Platonism which had a lasting influence on later Western thought, those of Augustine and the Pseudo-Dionysius.[20]

Augustine
In the sacramental thought of St. Augustine, memory and word play the key parts, and his vision of the effects of sin on nature is integral. There are some magnificent passages in Augustine's tracts on John's gospel wherein he lauds the mystery of the Word in whose image the human person is created, who descended from heaven on humanity's loss of this image, and who ascended anew to God's right hand as head of a refashioned and redeemed humanity.[21] This is what is approached by faith in liturgy, what is contemplated and celebrated therein. Through creation all things manifest the divine, and in creation and history Augustine invites his hearers or readers to see the traces of the Trinity. His work *The City of God* is a *tour de force* whereby all history is interpreted in relation to Jesus Christ and divine creation or

providence. Because sin corrupts humanity's vision and creation's power to represent, the word of revelation is necessary to bring the vision of Christ and God to thought.

Since the human person is created in the image of the Word, self-knowledge through memory ought to lead to the knowledge and contemplation of the Word. Sin obscures the mind, however, and so the knowledge of the Word reflected in the soul requires the word of revelation and healing grace. Memory has to uncover the deviations of sin in a person's life before the image of God can appear clearly therein. Augustine never put his final trust in words themselves, but believed that they did their work when they led to repentance and to the silent contemplation of the Word revealed in the person's own soul.

Oddly enough, some of the strongest influence of Augustine on Latin sacramental thought comes from the repetition by later medieval writers of axioms and definitions found in his works.[22] Often misconstrued and taken out of context, they played a part in forging a theology that was far less appreciative of mystery, symbol, and memory than was Augustine. In particular, his defense of the truth of sacraments celebrated by unworthy ministers, as well as the medieval elaborations on the sacramental character traced back to his writings, were incorporated into a theology that showed little appreciation of the church as subject, agent, and representation in sacramental celebration. Instead, such principles were made tributary to a theology which put its major emphasis on the power given to ordained ministers, and treated all other members of the church as recipients rather than as active participants.

Pseudo-Dionysius[23]
The concept of hierarchy is the keystone for the thought of that person known to history as the Pseudo-

49

Dionysius, whose true identity remains unknown. This writer proposed a communication of the divinity along a descending scale, an emanation of the multiple forms of being, rank upon rank, all participating in God in descending degree. The lesser participations are those most accessible to the human person, but contemplation of the divine requires that one move upwards on the ladder of participation. Contemplation is thus achieved through a process of purification, illumination, and perfection, leading from a knowledge of the lesser to a knowledge of the higher. An important method in this process is the dialectic of dissimilar similitudes. That is to say, in those beings which participate in the divine, one must be conscious both of the similitude and of the difference. Being alert to the difference can actually occasion a leap of the mind to the perception of higher forms of participation.

The writer distinguished between a heavenly hierarchy of beings and an earthly one. They are related in that the earthly reflects the celestial. The earthly is located in the church, in which Pseudo-Dionysius finds a twofold hierarchy, the one pertaining to spiritual perfection, the other to ministerial activity. The hierarchy of perfection is that of monks, laypersons, and catechumens. The ministerial hierarchy is the triad of bishop, presbyter, and deacon. It is the role of this latter hierarchy to serve the needs of the hierarchy of perfection, for it is the divine design and the nature of participation in the celestial hierarchy that the more active forms of participation should exercise an influence upon the more passive.

When the work of the Pseudo-Dionysius was assimilated into a later medieval vision of church and sacrament, three things in particular became important. First, the vision of the universe as hierarchical provided strong support for a hierarchical vision of the church, and of the sacraments as actions performed by the clergy for the other members. John the Scot enunciated the principle that the terrestrial hierarchy was not a hierarchy of beings but a multiplicity of formative activities. There was no risk of emanationism in such an adoption of the Pseudo-Dionysius, although the reflection of one universe in another remains in the distinction of activities and orders.

Second, Western theologians seemed peculiarly fascinated by the earlier writer's persuasion that in the dialectic of dissimilar similitude the grosser symbols had an advantage, since they were more prone to demand the leap to a higher realm, having little appeal in themselves for the human imagination. This meant that they could both draw attention to the use in Christian liturgy of gross and simple things such as bread, water, oil, and fire, and yet spend little time elaborating on their innate symbolism in favor of alerting readers to the divine action present through their use.

Third, symbolism could be indulged to a great extent in the explanation of the scriptures or in describing places and persons, and architecture abounded in the representational and the fanciful. Since there was little sense of reality being symbolic and participatory, however, the symbolic mode of discourse became more and more allegorical. In other words, rather than explaining the symbolism inherent in things from nature or history, writers used allegory as a device to draw attention away from things in themselves to a contemplation of higher beings and mysteries.

MEDIEVAL WESTERN THOUGHT
Medieval Western thought, even when it assimilated elements from the neo-Platonism of the patristic era, gradually lost touch with its underpinning of symbolic perception. It turned instead to a strong distinction between sign and reality and to a treatment of the

church which gave primary place to institutional factors and to a hierarchical model. This trend has both practical and theoretical background and substance.

The practical background is the liturgical development which left the laity as spectators of a clerical celebration or recipients of priestly administrations. Since their role was one of viewing and receiving, their needs were often met by putting an accent on the visual and on dramatization. The beginnings of dramatization are actually found in the patristic era, as for example in some passages of the mystagogical catechesis to which reference has already been made. This is particularly true of the work of Theodore of Mopsuestia, in which we find comments such as the following on the presentation of the gifts of bread and wine at the eucharist: "By means of signs we must see Christ being led away to his passion and again later when he is stretched out on the altar to be immolated for us."[24] This kind of dramatic explanation of the liturgy was rendered popular in the expositions on the Mass, of which the best known is that of Amalar of Metz.[25] It had its counterpart in the actual celebration of liturgy, ranging from a simple dramatization of some of the actions performed by clerics to a kind of staging of gospel proclamation in the divine office. An instance of the latter was the performance of Easter Vespers which developed to the extent that deacons played the roles of the women visiting the sepulcher, permitting the people to see what was being proclaimed in the gospel story.[26] The main defect in this trend is that representation takes over from symbolism. That is to say, events or mysteries were portrayed in order to teach and to arouse devotion. Signs or actions thus interpreted or used became reminders which spurred belief and feeling, rather than symbols in which events and mysteries were believed to be rendered present. The emphasis of the Middle Ages on the visual is well known, with its proliferation of relics and eucharistic devotions. Not all of this is to be spurned in the name of greater sophistication, for much of it did indeed have great potential. Thus the *biblia pauperum* of stained glass and fresco was a way of making the Bible known to people who could not read at all or did not know the biblical languages. Likewise, mystery plays, which probably had some basis in the dramatization of the gospel and other scriptures in the liturgy, could bring some of the catharsis which is an essential part of configuring one's life to an ideal. However, the clerics seem to have been unable to change liturgy itself in ways that integrated forms appropriate to culture and popular piety, so that it was often made accessible to people only through vulgarizations connected with the real presence, with relics, and with processions.

It is on the practical level that distinctions seem to have first occurred between sign and reality, which made signs a form of illustration and the reality totally obscure, known only by an act of belief which defied the perceptions of sense.[27] People were often denied the evidence of sacramental symbols which served to reveal or unveil the mystery, but might be comforted by visions or stories of the miraculous. The question was thus asked whether the body of Christ is present in the eucharist in figure or in truth, and over a few centuries the issue was forced to become a choice between one or the other. Even when writers answered that the body was present in both ways, they did not establish a clear connection between the two types of presence. The figure was not presented as one which served to reveal or to bring to the truth, but rather as a means of veiling the mystery or reality it contained. People were thus exhorted to believe in what was veiled, rather than taught about mysteries through an exploration of the symbols wherein they are revealed. The faithful were told by their instructors to believe what authority affirmed, and weak faith was bolstered, if at all, not by the persuasiveness of the symbolic but by miracle stories wherein it was recounted how an infant appeared in the monstrance, or blood dripped from the host, or the blood of a martyr liquified in its reliquary.

On the theoretical plane, Aristotelian metaphysics made a claim for investigation into the form and reality of things in themselves, without immediate reference to the divine reality of which patristic neo-Platonism had seen them as participating. Thus the presence of Christ in the sacraments at first seemed to be jeopardized, since it was acknowledged that the appearance of bread suggested its substance, as the appearance of water suggested water rather than divine instrumentality. How could the reality of sacrament be the body of Christ or his grace when appearances suggested otherwise? Such questions were answered by a theology of consecration and a deft use of analogy, particularly on the part of Thomas Aquinas. The theology of consecration worked out of a clear distinction between the sacred and the profane. This went with an appreciation of the reality of the natural order, which contained its own forms and not only those of a higher order. Matter was allowed to be changed into the holy through an exercise of divine power, inherent in the words used by ordained ministers. Analogy with things of the natural order could be used to explain what took place in the sacramental. The best known of these analogies is that used by Thomas Aquinas to explain the change of eucharistic bread and wine into the body and blood of Christ by way of analogy with the change of one substance into another in the natural order.[28] Aquinas' explanation was subtle enough to avoid any confusion between these two orders or to avoid any suggestion of a physical rather than a sacramental presence of Christ, but its vulgarization in later centuries did not respect these subtleties.

The major problem with this type of explanation was that it failed to give a good account of the function of sign in explaining sacraments and liturgy, a difficulty which paralleled one that occurred in explaining the spiritual sense of the scriptures. It was explained that divine power could change the reality of things in the sacramental order, and that divine revelation could also attach a significance to things and persons which they did not of themselves possess. In liturgy there was some parallel between the operation of divine power and the significance of the holy attached to things and words, but there was little explanation which showed an intrinsic connection between these two. This meant that liturgical signs did not teach much of themselves, for they could only illustrate what one already knew by authority. Indeed, any sign which seemed to be peculiarly apt to teach of mystery was not of itself a guarantee of the presence of mystery. Representation was not seen to bring about presence; presence depended on the exercise of priestly power. Within such a compass of thought, Aquinas could compare the presence of Christ's passion in the Mass to the presence of Cicero in a portrait without affirming the presence of this passion in mystery, but at the same time explain that the Mass did give the grace of the passion through the exercise of priestly power.[29]

A rather typical text for these times is the following from Hugo of St. Victor, in which he explains that something can be both sign and reality, when the sign comes from a similitude and the reality is guaranteed by divine power:

"Is the sacrament of the altar not truth, because it is a sign? Then neither is Christ's death, because that is a sign, nor his resurrection, because that too is a sign. The Apostle clearly states that Christ's death and resurrection is a sign, a similitude, a representation, a sacrament, an example: Christ died for our sins and rose again for our justification [Rom. 4.25]. . . . Cannot the sacrament of the altar be a similitude *and* also a truth?"[30]

In this text, the similitude that Hugo is writing about is the Pasch; the truth is the reality of the body and blood. In a like manner, the death and resurrection are the similitude and our justification the truth. Note how he separates reality and similitude, for the truth and reality are one thing, the similitude is another. Along with the reality of the body and the blood in the eucharist, it is possible to have a representation or similitude of the passion. In the celebration of the eucharist one can elaborate the representation of the passion because one is sure of the presence of the body and blood which can be reverenced and received in communion.

In the elaboration of similitudes or representations, Hugo used the exegetical principle of their reference to scriptural history. Through a proper use of the scriptures one could use symbols and images to demonstrate invisible truth. In presenting the spiritual sense of the scriptures, Hugo expected proper respect for the literal meaning, just as for sacramental symbols he gave explanations which respected the nature of the things spoken of as representative. This curbed flights of fancy in interpretation, but nonetheless established the principle of allegorical interpretation, a principle not as soberly used by other allegorists. The allegorical principle allows expositors to look to things or words as illustrations of another truth or reality. It is different from the sacramental principle, which allows one to look to symbols for a revelation of the truth present in them as in a distinct mode of being.

It has already been mentioned how Western thought on sacrament related to the neo-Platonism of Augustine and the Pseudo-Dionysius. How it used symbolic representation can therefore be summarized.

First, it distinguished sharply between sign and reality, so that the connection between the two became tenuous. Second, it adopted and formalized a hierarchical vision of church and sacramental celebration. Third, it opened the way for a great stress on the visual and on the allegorical in fostering the participation of the faithful, and allowed an increasing separation between popular piety and liturgical celebration.

CONCLUSION

This chapter has done little more than present in sharp outline the development of thought from the early age of Christianity to the medieval West, mainly the move from an age in which symbolic thought prevailed to one marked by a popular naive realism and a theoretical separation between reality and sign. There was also a move from the desacralizing tendencies of the New Testament period to a resacralization that was occasioned by both practical and theoretical currents. Understanding these developments prepares one to better grasp the issues that are debated today and the current changes in practice.

NOTES

1. John E. Burkhart, *Worship* (Philadelphia: Westminster Press, 1982); Ferdinand Hahn, *The Worship of the Early Church* (Philadelphia: Fortress Press, 1973).

2. F. Gavin, *The Jewish Antecedents of the Christian Eucharist* (New York: KTAV, 1969); W.O.E. Oesterly, *The Jewish Background of the Christian Liturgy* (New York: Oxford University Press, 1925).

3. On the cross in early Christianity, see Hans Ruedi-Weber, *The Cross: Tradition and Interpretation* (Grand Rapids, Mich.: Eerdmans, 1979).

4. A. Hamman, "La résurrection du Christ dans l'antiquité Chrétienne," *Revue des Sciences Religieuses* 50 (1976), 1–24; P. Pokorný, "Christologie et baptême à l'epoque du Christianisme primitif," *New Testament Studies* 27 (1981), 368–80.

5. Joachim Jeremias, *The Eucharistic Words of Jesus* (Philadelphia: Fortress Press, 1977).

6. Robert J. Daly, *Christian Sacrifice: The Judaeo-Christian Background before Origen* (Washington, D.C.: Catholic University of America Press, 1978), pp. 240–60, 276–84; R. Corriveau, *The Liturgy of Life: A Study of the Ethical Thought of St. Paul in His Letters to the Early Christian Communities* (Brussels-Montreal: Bellarmin, 1970).

7. J. Z. Smith, *Map is Not Territory. Studies in the History of Religions,* Studies in Judaism in Late Antiquity 36 (Leiden: Brill, 1978).

8. Jacob Neusner, "Map without territory: Mishnah's system of sacrifice and sanctuary," *History of Religions* 19 (1979), 103–27.

9. Brevard Childs, *Memory and Tradition in Israel* (Naperville, Tenn.: Allenson, 1962).

10. X. Léon-Dufour, "Das letzte Mahl Jesu und die testamentarische Tradition nach Lk. 22," *Zeitschrift für Katholische Theologie* 103 (1981), 33–55.

11. *Baptism, Eucharist and Ministry,* Faith and Order Paper No. 111 (Geneva: World Council of Churches, 1982), pp. 15–16.

12. See Robert Taft, in a book review in *Worship* 56 (1982), 178: "Comparative anaphoral studies will yield no secure results until much more work has been done on the roots of our early sources, especially in those traditions that refuse to fit into the ever-so-neat Antiochene patterns favored by composers of contemporary eucharistic prayers."

13. Brian Spinks, "The anaphora for India: Some theological objections to an attempt of inculturation," *Ephemerides Liturgicae* 95 (1981), 529–49. On the history and principles of

adaptation, see Anscar J. Chupungco, *Cultural Adaptation of the Liturgy* (New York: Paulist, 1982).

14. See the issue entitled *God as Father?*, *Concilium* 143 (Edinburgh: Clark, 1981).

15. For a convenient English translation, see Edward Yarnold, *The Awe Inspiring Rites of Initiation: Baptismal Homilies of the Fourth Century* (Slough: St. Paul Publications, 1971). For extensive commentary, see Hugh M. Riley, *Christian Initiation* (Washington, D.C.: Catholic University of America Press, 1974).

16. Aidan Kavanagh, *The Shape of Baptism: The Rite of Christian Initiation* (New York: Pueblo, 1978), pp. 3–78.

17. This is no more than an oblique reference to the relation between liturgical development and popular religion, a study which is fast developing a whole library unto itself.

18. R. Gryson, *Les Origines du Célibat Ecclésiastique du premier au septième siècle* (Gembloux: Duculot, 1970).

19. D. Holeton, "The sacramental language of St. Leo the Great. A study of the words 'munus' and 'oblata,' " *Ephemerides Liturgicae* 92 (1978), 115–65.

20. These are conveniently summarized in M. D. Chenu, *Nature, Man and Society in the Twelfth Century*, selected, edited and translated by Jerome Taylor and Lester K. Little (Chicago: University of Chicago Press, 1979), pp. 49–98.

21. See for example the homilies on John VI; Augustine of Hippo, *Homilies on the Gospel According to St. John and His First Epistle*, vol. 1, translated with notes and indices (Oxford: John Henry Parker, 1848), pp. 372–425.

22. N. M. Häring, "St. Augustine's use of the word character," *Medieval Studies* 14 (1952), 79–97; and "Berengar's definitions of sacramentum and their influence on medieval sacramentology," *Medieval Studies* 10 (1948), 109–46.

23. Dionysius the Pseudo-Areopagite, *The Ecclesiastical Hierarchy*, translated and annotated by Thomas L. Campbell (Washington, D.C.: University Press of America, 1981).

24. Yarnold, p. 227.

25. I. M. Hanssens (ed.), *Liber Officialis* (Vatican City: Vatican Press, 1948).

26. Blandine-Dominique Berger, *Le Drame Liturgique de Pâques: Liturgie et Théatre* (Paris: Beauchesne, 1976); O. B. Hardison, *Christian Rite and Christian Drama in the Middle Ages* (Baltimore: Johns Hopkins University Press, 1965).

27. Nathan Mitchell, *Cult and Controversy: The Worship of the Eucharist Outside Mass* (New York: Pueblo, 1982), pp. 10–196.

28. *Summa Theologiae III*, Q. 75.

29. *Summa Theologiae III*, Q. 83, art. 1.

30. *De Sacramentis Christianae Fidei*, i. 8, vi. 466, as quoted in Beryl Smalley, *The Study of the Bible in the Middle Ages* (Notre Dame, Ind.: University of Notre Dame Press, 1970), p. 93.

Chapter Three

Symbol Described

In relating symbol to sacrament and liturgy, it is
common to work with some traditional definition of
sign, such as that given by St. Augustine that a sign
"leads to knowledge of something other than itself,"[1]
and then to add to this, on the basis of the etymology
sum-ballein (to throw together), that symbols make
present the things that they signify and thus allow
communion with them.

Such observations have their utility, but a more
thorough investigation of liturgy as symbolic requires
considerable attention to the complexity of this field.
This is reflected in the different approaches taken by
those who discuss symbol in a concerted way, whether
in theology, philosophy, poetics, sociology,
anthropology, psychology, or the history of religions.[2]
To introduce the subject, we can begin with what looks
like a pragmatic definition offered by Antoine Vergote,
one that is inclusive of "perceptual, affective, linguistic,
social, cultural and historical dimensions":

"A symbol is a concrete sign, or a concrete gesture or
action: first, that man receives from his cultural
environment and appropriates in a more or less active
way or even creative manner; second, that serves him
in all reference systems; third, in which he expresses
himself and in which he recognizes, explicitly or
implicitly, an essential part of his personal, cultural,
familial, social and eventually religious identity; and,

fourth, that links him with some group that shares this identity."[3]

Putting the element of the religious in brackets for the moment, this pragmatic definition can be applied to sundry things, such as a national flag, receiving the car keys at age eighteen, commemoration ceremonies, academic graduations, initiation rites, the cross, shaking hands, or giving an accolade. Obviously, these are not all of equal importance, but they all belong within a given cultural context, bear of repetition without being rigid stereotypes, meet affective needs of meaning and belonging, express group identity, even though some are more immediately related to the group and others to the individual, and are subject to the changes that come with the evolution of time, moving perspectives, and changing values.

The things that are used, done, and said in liturgy fall under this description. Bread and wine, oil and water, standing and kneeling, thanking and invoking, do not invent their meaning every time they are employed, though each occasion can give to them a distinctive shade of meaning dependent on immediate circumstances. Those who take part regularly in liturgical celebrations regard this as essential to their well-being and find in this activity a point of reference in all companies, situations, and contexts of any moment. They know that liturgy defines them as people who belong to a particular group of persons, who have their own view of life and its meaning. It is well to keep this pragmatic and rather general description of symbol in mind when treating specific questions that lead to a fuller understanding.

SIGN AND SYMBOL
Symbols fall within the general category of signs because their whole existence has to do with something other than themselves. Yet a difference exists between

signs used for functional and organizational purposes and those which touch on the meaning of things. Nobody confuses mathematical symbols with cultural rites, nor street indicators with the decorations put up as part of investiture ceremonies. Symbols in the cultural sense have to do with the world as meaningful, whereas the kind of signs from which they are separated have to do with making living in the world functional.

One suspects that the two somehow coalesce, however, which means that the distinction is not as clear cut as it seems at first. For all its practicality in a motorist's handbook, meanings other than functional are concealed in the classification of some roads as highways, others as avenues, and others as side streets. The classification also defines space, grades social importance, classifies the places where people live or work, maps out territory, and in all of this says something about the values and purposes that the population pursues. The reverse observation is also true: what is primarily symbolic, that is, concerning significance and meaning, also concerns the functionality of knowing things apart. Designating one person as minister in a ceremony is indicative of the performance that is expected of that person, as well as of the meaning attached to the role. Asking whether or not bread has been consecrated is not a sign of superstition, but the request for a practical knowledge without which specific religious acts do not have the space to be performed.

Any word, thing, or action can bear a variety of meanings, their significance determined by context. At first hearing, a word such as "house" seems to designate only one kind of thing, but then we hear the expression "to build a house" used to mean something done in the builders' trade, to suggest the prolongation of a dynasty, or to betoken a spiritual attitude, as in the psalm which says that "unless the Lord build the house, those labor in vain who build it." Eating designates a bodily function, but no one is surprised to hear someone say she could eat her words, or to be told of a financial loss eating into profits.

There are three contexts in which the lexical significance of words, or the primary nature of things and actions, receives determination of meaning and designation.[4] The first context is that of ordinary, every-day affairs. Here people are concerned to deal with situations and interact among themselves in commonsense, practical fashion, and so eliminate ambiguity as far as possible. In this world, it is preferable for words, things, and actions to have clear purposes and meanings. A jug is meant to hold liquids, a knife to cut, announcement of the time to eat is clearly an invitation or an order to sit down to dinner, and calling someone son or daughter leaves no doubt about the nature of the relationship.

In the second context, the world of science, meanings are more abstract in character, but they are still clearly and technically defined. Equivocity or polysemy is not considered a virtue. Mathematical symbols, the naming of chemical elements, types of experiments, the forms of logical reasoning, all eradicate multiplicity of meanings as far as possible, because the world ruled by science and technology runs better when meanings and uses are fixed.

In contrast to both of these uses of signs and language, the world of the symbol, the third context, intentionally deploys the multiple possibilities of meaning. A flag flying on top of a building recalls past history, evokes in the passersby a sense of national pride, and reveals that Parliament is in session, all at once. In this case, although the immediately obvious functional indication is that the country's legislators have not gone home, the whole setting is symbolic in intent. In other cases the functional does not enter at all except within the compass of the ritual, as when a flag is lowered at the sounding of the last post.

In the liturgy, a symbolic use is intended, although a factual, commonsense designation is in many instances necessary for the participants, and the technical easily intrudes on it in an effort to pin down meanings. In the eucharist, the word and thing "bread" must have a demonstrable reference to what common sense recognizes as such a substance, but its meaning in the ceremony depends on its cultural and traditional polysemy. Bread feeds, but it also gathers. It may be taken or it may be given. There is the bread that nourishes, the bread that delights, and the bread of affliction. In the tradition there is the bread that David took from the tabernacle, the bread of manna in the desert, the bread of the Jewish Pasch, the bread that Jesus broke with his disciples, and the bread that he promised for the life of the world. Liturgy suffers when an effort is made to tie down the meaning. When the bread of the Lord's Supper functioned only as a thing to be swallowed, but not broken, chewed, or shared, when the semantic context referred to it only as the body of Christ to be eaten or adored, the richness of multiple meanings was lost. Similar remarks could be made about water, oil, rings, books, and candles.

DOUBLE MEANING[5]
Meaning is determined in the poetic and symbolic context by the use of double meaning, whereby the second meaning is given in the first by reason of the new context. Although words, things, and actions are patient of a variety of meanings, or can even be said to contain them embryonically, the number of these is neither arbitrary nor infinite. The meanings given in any context are bound to the nature of a thing, the bodily function of an action, and the place in the language code of a word. The ordinary, every-day

meaning or meanings are determined in this way and remain operative in the symbolic context. When one of these every-day meanings is transferred to the symbolic context, the capacity of word, thing, or action to signify something about the meaning of life or the world appears. In this properly symbolic context, the second or symbolic meaning is given in the first. There is nothing arbitrary to the attachment of the symbolic meaning, except when poetic speech degenerates to allegory, and the symbolic meaning is given only to those who attend to the every-day meaning. Thus when moral evil is spoken of as blemish, this is no allegorical predication meant to illustrate what is already known, but the nature of moral evil and its experience is articulated and revealed in the use of the image of blemish in a moral and religious context. That this is then complemented by the use of other images does not mean an error in the image of blemish, but is accounted for by the complex nature of the experience of evil.[6]

Other examples abound in liturgy where this same donation of second meaning through the first occurs. Breaking bread is an action of dividing and sharing, which done in a memorial of Christ's death reveals some part of its meaning. Anointing a sick person has healing and soothing qualities to it, which affect the senses of touch and smell, and in this action the Lord's healing power, alive in the community's compassion, is expressed and offered.

Faced with the richness of sacramental signs, there is a triple tendency to falsify this movement of double meaning. The first tendency is to refuse the interplay of images, to concentrate, for example, only on the moment of marriage when promises are exchanged. The second is to impose defined, technical meanings on words and actions, using them only as allegory, as occasions of indoctrination, or at best as illustrations of concepts and effects. This is a move associated with instrumental action, typical of control systems and domination of some by others. The third tendency is to resort to picturing, to the naive realism which confuses the symbolic meaning with the every-day, so that one remains in the world of immediate sense perceptions.

Any attempt to reduce the signification of liturgical symbols and speech to a single or preconceived meaning thwarts their efficacy. Discursive reasoning may indeed pick out some focal meaning which gives valuable insight into what the church does at liturgy and how it relates to God, but this can be balanced with other meanings and complemented by them. Discussions about the primary meaning of anointing, whether it is to prepare for death or to give the strength of witness in illness, are not misplaced and rightly appeal to a tradition. Yet, it is an impoverishment when a community fails to remember in this context the oil which anointed priests, kings, prophets, and martyrs, the naming of Jesus as the Anointed One, the uses of oil in healing and nourishing, and its poetic connotation of the abundance of the land. Even more fundamentally, it is not unimportant to reflect on whether the focal meaning of Jesus' death is testimony or passing over, and on what this says about human creatureliness, about redemption, and about God's presence to the world. The history and theology of liturgy are reminders, however, that even when the focal meaning seems clear for a period, a return to the polysemy of the symbol can give rise to fresh discursive thinking. In this return to symbol and symbolic tradition, it must be asked constantly how much the donation of the second meaning in the first has been forgotten or neglected, and what thought can arise from a fresh perception of the process.

This distinction between the commonsense, scientific, and poetic contexts within which words, things, and actions are given determined meanings may more readily get to the heart of the distinction between sign (or signal) and symbol. As used by Susanne Langer, the distinction between signal and symbol puts them both into the genus of sign.[7] The signal is not intended to make something more intelligible or affect attitudes or feelings toward anything. Like smoke, it says simply that something else lurks in the vicinity and this knowledge demands a reaction. It is an indication or warning, like a bell ringing for dinner, a siren clearing the road for an ambulance, an angry dog reminding that intrusion is not welcome. This corresponds to the ordinary, every-day, commonsense use of language that makes it possible to get from morning to night without starving to death, being run down by a car, or mistaking the police station for the tax consultant's office. However, concentrating on a clear-cut distinction between signal and symbol could make us forget the residual, unattended symbolism latent in any word or thing, however commonplace. Langer is aware of this aspect of signals. She points out that sense perceptions and the most unreflective images provide what she calls "symbolic materials," so that her distinction is a functional rather than an ontological one.

Langer treats of symbols in terms of a process of symbolization which she deems absolutely necessary for the human being's access to, and understanding of, reality. Her definitions of symbols are given in terms of understanding, but her explanations indicate that, for her, understanding is inclusive of feeling and value perception. Thus, she says that the prime office of symbols is "their power of formulating experience, and presenting it objectively for contemplation, logical intuition, recognition, understanding."[8] Symbols by nature take hold of experience and give it form and expression in such a way that it becomes accessible to thought. Symbols are an abstraction and liberate thought from immersion in the immediately present physical world.

Langer distinguishes between discursive and presentational symbols, rather than between concept and symbol, because all thought is tied to language of some sort. Language penetrates all human cerebral activity, fantasy and memory, intuition and dreaming, distinguishing and relating. None of this activity is possible without language and other forms of creative, rather than instinctive, expression. Discursive symbols are those which divide in order to conquer, which separate things from one another, which allow us to pass from one act of understanding to another while keeping the two distinct. For Langer this is the language used in science and philosophy, and that makes definition and explanation possible. Presentational symbols on the other hand occur in a simultaneous, integral expression, the purpose of which is to allow thoughts and things to interpenetrate, to come together so that the whole is perceived as one, and to express, as distinct from scientific understanding, the kind of understanding associated with feelings and values, or what is called aesthetic appreciation.

In these distinctions, Langer indicates that it is the human operation that makes the difference between signal and symbol, between discursive and presentational symbols, rather than words or images in themselves. The distinction between the ordinary, scientific, and poetic contexts within which language operates allows a better grasp of the natural symbolic or polysemic quality of language, of the ways in which this is at work unconsciously even in commonsense approaches and in theory, and of the human need to address oneself to the reality of the world, and humankind's dwelling in it, in distinct but interconnected ways. In other words, this distinction is true to the fundamental polysemy of every image, word, thing, or action, to the nature of knowledge as originally symbolic, to the structure of being that is revealed in the capacity for multiple significance and multiple reference of language, and to the human need for a multiple relation to reality that is practical, theoretical, and reverential.

PRESENCE AND ABSENCE

Because symbolic or poetic language is reverential and nondiscursive, and because it embraces feelings and values as well as insight into meaning, it is used in contexts where communion and communication of an interpersonal nature is intended.[9] It also makes present realities not present in their own specific form of being and expression. This can at times be affirmed with a flourish of rhetoric in the interests of persuasiveness, as when it is said that the Lord's Supper makes present the body and blood of Jesus Christ, or that the priest represents Christ in the community. The danger is that in the flourish it may be forgotten that the presence is given in a foreign form, one made necessary by the otherly character of those put into communication. When this is forgotten, the imagination goes to work and forces the image only of a *hidden* reality, neglecting the concomitant qualities of absence and separation that go with being present in symbol. In the Lord's Supper, one then imagines Jesus hidden behind or underneath the appearance of bread. In baptism one imagines the removal of a stain that makes one displeasing.

While the affective, interpersonal, and communicatory nature of symbolic exchange is rightly affirmed,[10] its usage has to embrace negativity and the nonidentity between the symbol and reality.[11] A good way to understand the use of symbolic language is to reflect on what it takes to understand oneself or to possess oneself. The human person does not gain knowledge of the self through a simple process of introspection. Self-knowledge is mediated by a projection into images, language, and action—most of which are provided by others or by the culture and society of which one is a part, even if for each person they have their own distinctive peculiarity in the way they are appropriated for self-expression. Images, language, and action are not the whole self, but they are the necessary way to self-knowledge. They can be compared to a mirror which reflects the person back to the self, but they are illusory if the image is confused with the self. This expression is also a necessary condition for communicating with other persons. Neither self-knowledge nor exchange is realized if the person does not accept the nonidentity between the expression and the expressed, and so accept in communication between persons the element of absence of the other in the very mode of presence.

It is possible to go beyond these examples of self-knowledge and interpersonal exchange, and to see that it is in the very nature of being, a quality of all reality, that it can be appreciated only when it comes to expression in symbolic or poetic language, even though this paradoxically veils its nature as well as reveals it. The nature of bread is revealed when it is broken, shared, offered, and praised in poem and song. In acts of worship and sacrament, it is wonderful to realize that the things of nature and human artifacts are not simply being put to use for a purpose, but that their very nature is being revealed within such acts.

The dynamic involved in embracing the negativity as well as the revelation is expressed by writers in various ways, such as going from image to symbol, from the symbolic to the symbol, or in the metaphor of breaking images. The nature of symbolization is not to be reduced to picturing, but is to be taken as the drive toward the one and the true and the good which remains conscious of the nonidentity of the symbol with these transcendentals. In keeping with this nonidentity, reality is not expressed in a single image but in what can be called an image-schema or a symbol system, where various images and symbols coalesce.

In the case of sacrament or liturgical action, no one image does duty for the Lord's presence and for the memory of his passion. The symbols of his presence in the sacramental action are inseparable from those of his presence in the community, and the symbols of the Lord's presence are complemented by the symbols of the presence of the Spirit. Furthermore, the iconic representation and the ritual action are inseparable from the narrative and the act of praise. The image-schema is made up of a plurality of referents and forms of representation, brought together by the work of ecclesial imagination, which is recognized as the communal and public work of the believing community. Liturgy does not deal with what goes on in an individual's fantasy, but with something that the church assembly recognizes as its own, whatever the individual talents that together bring it to being. The church celebrates the presence of its Lord in these symbols, while at the same time recognizing the absence that will endure until the eschaton.

SYMBOLS AND THE AFFECTIVE

Through the bodily, we gain entry into our different worlds, the social, cultural, moral, aesthetic, and interpersonal. It is to the root relation of our being to bios and cosmos that the psychic and the affective are related. Symbols both explore and transform this element of experience, in conjunction with their exploration and transformation of intelligible meaning and desirable value. Cognition and value are in fact inseparable from the psychic and affective. Human presence in reality is both cognitive and affective, the two being intertwined, and as there is differentiation in the cognitive modes so too there is in the affective. For example, symbols which posit meaning more in the internal than in the external, or that are more concerned with the sacredness of history than with the sacredness of places, not only have cognitive implications but also have affective resonances. When people cease to represent reality by picturing and so differentiate between images and symbols, not only their world of conceived meaning is touched but also their affective relationships, their dispositions of belonging, awe, and respect, and their sense of personal wholeness and of oneness with the world.

Writers on symbolism have learned much about the affective and psychic roots of symbolism from Freud and Jung, and the contributions of psychoanalysis continue to be explored. While it is said that Freud remained too etiological in his exploration of the origins of psychic disturbances and in his evaluation of the effects of the psyche on culture,[12] Jung is accounted to have taken more seriously the teleological nature of the psyche and so to have found therein the roots of the desire for communion with the awesome and the transcendent. Robert Doran has pointed out,[13] within a schema of Lonerganian method, several aspects of Jung's theory that help in grasping the relation between symbol and the affective. Doran points out on his reading of Jung that conscious intentionality is always in commerce with a fund of symbolic meanings, which Jung associated with the archetypal and the personal memory. Human development requires that the person keep in touch with this source, and of course this also has implications for cultural symbol systems. The differentiation of consciousness typical of the contemporary era has uprooted persons and civilizations from psychic roots and has made them suspicious of transcendental significations which appear to be explained by projection of the unconscious. Affective wholeness requires that we be ready to encounter the darkness which comes with this awareness of the psychic roots of the symbolic. This darkness comes not only from what we fail as yet to discern either in the personal or in the collective unconscious, but also from what we know about them. Such knowledge can readily cast doubt on beliefs and belief systems, if they are seen as projections of the transcendental or teleological drive of the unconscious. When symbols address themselves more explicitly to interiority, can they also address themselves to the awareness of these affective drives, associating them with the quest for the truth and the good? In this connection, Doran believes[14] that Jung ended up wanting to explain too much. Jung looked for wholeness in a continuing search for further differentiation of the unconscious, whereas the darkness of knowledge of self and of the collective that comes with the light shed by psychology can be met only by recognizing the transcendent power and finality that are not within the compass of the human person or the human race. Explorations of the unconscious do not bring perfect knowledge, nor the ultimate possibility of reconciliation with self, reconciliation with the body and with the cosmos, or reconciliation with the race. This can be attained only by those who place themselves before the transcendent, the ultimate source of being and reconciliation. Therefore, on the affective level, symbols speak to internal conflict, internal drives, and internal hopes, to the need for communion with the body and with the cosmos. They offer wholeness within a system that demands faith in the transcendent.

SYMBOLS OF THE HOLY
Cultural differences show up markedly in symbols of the holy, as do clashes within cultures and in cultural approaches to Christianity. Their place within a cultural symbol system relates to the cohesiveness of that system. When the holy becomes privatized or marginal

to the major interests of life, this constitutes a major cultural change. As Clifford Geertz puts it:

"Sacred symbols relate an ontology and a cosmology to an aesthetics and a morality: their peculiar power comes from their presumed ability to identify fact with value at the most fundamental level, to give to what is otherwise merely actual, a comprehensive normative import."[15]

Indeed, where sacred symbols or belief in a transcendent power is dismissed from contemporary ideologies, as in Marxism or liberal progressivism, students of these systems look for some other appeal to permanent order and meaning.[16] However, let us remain here within the compass of the holy. Two qualities are observed in what symbols of the holy signify about that to which they attribute ultimate significance—for example in designating places and times, persons or actions, as holy. First, in terms now often borrowed from Rudolf Otto,[17] they represent the holy as wholly other, a *mysterium tremendum et fascinans*. It is *tremendum* because it inspires awe, even dread and fear. It is *fascinans* because it attracts, enraptures, and promises happiness through communion with it. The second note of the holy evoked by its symbols is its ultimacy and ability to grant wholeness to persons and societies who acknowledge it as the supreme and ultimate power in human life.

In representations of the holy, there is an interplay between hierophany, word, and silence. Cultural approaches to the holy retain elements of all three, but the differences between cultures appear in the predominance given to one or another of the three kinds of expression. Silence has never had the importance in Christianity that it has for example in Buddhism,[18] except in some forms of mysticism where the negativity of being and the nonidentity of God with representations are stressed. Therefore, it is enough here to discuss the symbolism of the holy in hierophany and in word.[19]

Hierophany as a mode of sacred revelation attaches primordial importance to the nonverbal, to sacred places and times, to sacred representations, to things infused with sacred power, to the iconic and the visually aesthetic. Preference for the hierophanic entails doubt about the verbal, since the power of mystery cannot be expressed in human language and the cosmos is more expressive of divine awesomeness than is the human tongue. Ritual actions express a way of being in time and place which conforms to the sacred. According to this mode, the sacred has a logic which expresses correspondence between a celestial model and that which is held sacred on earth, whether it be the ways in which the sacred is manifested or the life of a holy person. Cosmic rhythm and bodily rhythm are related, so that seasonal rites and rites of human passage have great importance. Even word use is conformed to this model and to the supremacy of the nonverbal, in the form of myths which tell the story of the life of the otherworldly in ways that promote its imitation and its reenactment in ritual.

Where word has first place in the expression of the holy, the nonverbal comes under suspicion. Revelation is believed to have its singularity in discourse rather than in the numinous suggested by holy places, times, things, and actions. The historical factor is taken to determine the presence of the holy. This puts cosmic order, or the relation between myths and rites, into disarray. Word in its various forms, such as narrative, myth, parable, prophecy, and proverb, is held better able to signify the nonidentity of the divine with its manifestations. The paradoxes of word and the iconoclasm of word are said to enter into dialectic with hierophany.

Those who look to the root of the transcendental in human consciousness and experience believe that the primacy given to word is more in keeping with the Judeo-Christian tradition, although they do not deny the necessity of the dialectic just mentioned. In this age of the differentiation of consciousness and the crisis of the hierarchical, they look to the analysis of human experience for signals of the transcendent and for openings to a hearing of God's word. Thus some speak of limit-experiences, such as those which show the limits of human life in common experiences such as death, birth, or human tragedy, or those which in the very pursuit of human knowledge and human control show the limits to human capacity.[20] Those more politically minded look to the remembrance of the victims of human systems, to the memory of suffering, as a reminder that without a divine power, liberation and redemption are impossible, or that in the very paradox of suffering and death God's power and holiness are revealed.[21] In both cases, destruction of the supremacy of systems, which supremacy appears to be the temptation of the fascination with hierophany, is deemed in line with the Christian revelation of God.

Others believe that a renewal of hierophany is needed in a time of great loss of faith, and of a concomitant loss of communion with the cosmos and respect for human life. This renewal will come in the recovery of the permanent elements of myth and rite which have been assumed into Christian revelation, and of a sense of the aesthetic, especially in face of the mystery of the Word Incarnate. In particular, Hans Urs von Balthasar criticizes the theological approach to the transcendental which has its roots in an analysis of human experience and human intentionality for collapsing the distinctively Christian into claims for what are only exemplary illustrations of the human spirit's quest for God.[22] He sees the twin elements of love and the aesthetic as the guarantee of divine revelation and expression of God's holiness. Christ is known as Word of God in the love practiced among his disciples and in the aesthetic of his manifestation as divine image. The qualities of wholeness and integrity of form which philosophers associate with the beautiful are supremely manifest in historical revelation, which has its center in Christ, Word made flesh. The structure of that revelation is so profound and so complete that even death and suffering have their clear part in the pattern. God is known in Christ, not by analysis of the parts but in contemplation of the whole.

Following similar lines of thought, with particular reference to the church's liturgy, Louis Bouyer believes that in this secular, rationalistic age and in these postconciliar days for the church, retrieval of this aesthetic and contemplative model depends in large part on the retrieval of the liturgy's mythic and ritual elements.[23] These are the true antecedents to Christianity in other religions.[24] Their metamorphosis in the revelation of Christ as divine wisdom and eternal man, rather than an appeal to human experience and human word, constitutes the revelation of the holy in Christianity.

This clash of viewpoints within the church about symbols of the holy has important consequences for worship. On the one side, importance is given to word and to the church's ability in a poetics of word to express the contemporary human encounter with Christ. This viewpoint carries a sense of time and history which is teleological or eschatological, which looks to the future for the utopia of God's kingdom and celebrates this hope in liturgy. The aesthetics of this kind of worship is sensitive to the many forms of word in Bible and liturgy and practices the modes of irony that undo any tendencies toward absolute claims, religious or political. Within such a perspective, many sacramental elements are open to change, and cultural differences are considerable.

On the other side, more moment is given to the iconic, to the holiness of place and time, to the aura of the mysterious and numinous, and to permanent and unchanging elements in ritual celebration. Time and history are represented by images that conform to the spatial and the unchangeable.[25] The aesthetic is one of contemplation of the iconic, with emphasis on the visual and on the awe which it inspires, or on rites that represent divine mysteries. Cultural differences are certainly acknowledged, but certain elements are felt to defy change and allow for a certain transcultural uniformity.

CONCLUSION

In this chapter, a general overview of the nature and functioning of symbol has been sought, with the effects of this understanding on liturgy in mind. First, it was suggested that the distinctiveness of the symbolic in relation to other forms of language comes from context and usage rather than from an ontological difference between sign and symbol. Second, this was explained by way of symbol's use of double meaning. Third, the distinction made was compared with the distinction between signal and discursive and presentational symbols. Fourth, the negativity and nonidentity inherent in symbolic reference was discussed. Fifth, symbol's impact on affectivity was taken up. Finally, the chapter outlined approaches to symbols of the holy, with reference to the contemporary crisis in Western liturgy, associated with changes in cultural outlook.

In the next two chapters we will discuss in more detail the symbolic elements that are found in liturgy and that together constitute the symbolic universe of Christian belief.

NOTES

1. Augustine, *De Doctrina Christiana* II, 1:PL 34, 35.

2. J. Chevalier remarks "l'emploi du mot *symbole* révèle des variations de sens considérable"; Jean Chevalier & Alain Gheerbrant, *Dictionnaire des Symboles* (Paris: Seghers, 1973), p. xv. Paul Ricoeur finds that the difficulty in treating symbols is that they belong to too many and too diverse fields of research. See Paul Ricoeur, *Interpretation Theory* (Fort Worth: Texas Christian University Press, 1976), p. 53.

3. Antoine Vergote, Concluding Reflections, in "Religious symbolism and intercultural communication, an international seminar," *Kerygma* 14 (1980), 91. Clifford Geertz offers this definition of sacred symbols: "Sacred symbols relate an ontology and a cosmology to an aesthetics and a morality: their peculiar power comes from their presumed ability to identify fact with value at the most fundamental level, to give to what is otherwise merely actual, a comprehensive import"; "Ethos, World View, and the Analysis of Sacred Symbols," in *The Interpretation of Cultures* (New York: Basic Books, 1973), pp. 127–28.

4. Paul Ricoeur, "Creativity in language," *Philosophy Today* 17 (1973), 97–111.

5. Paul Ricoeur, "Existence and hermeneutics," in *The Conflict of Interpretations* (Evanston, Ill.: Northwestern University Press, 1974), pp. 11–24. On p. 12 he gives this definition: "I define symbol as: any structure of signification in which a direct, primary, literal meaning designates, in addition, another meaning which is indirect, secondary, and figurative and which can be apprehended only through the first."

6. Paul Ricoeur, *The Symbolism of Evil* (Boston: Beacon Press, 1967).

7. Susanne K. Langer, *Feeling and Form: A Theory of Art* (New York: Scribner's, 1953), p. 26.

8. Susanne K. Langer, *Problems of Art: Ten Philosophical Lectures* (New York: Scribner's, 1957), p. 130; *Philosophy in A New Key: A Study in the Symbolism of Reason, Rite, and Art*, 3rd ed. (Cambridge, Mass.: Harvard University Press, 1978), pp. 79–102.

9. Gibson Winter, *Liberating Creation: Foundations of Religious Social Ethics* (New York: Crossroad, 1981), pp. 29–91.

10. Louis-Marie Chauvet, *Du Symbolique au Symbole: Essai sur les Sacrements* (Paris: Cerf, 1979), pp. 37–79.

11. Ibid., 94–97.

12. Paul Ricoeur, *Freud and Philosophy: An Essay in Interpretation* (New Haven, Conn.: Yale University Press, 1970); "A philosophical interpretation of Freud," *The Conflict of Interpretations*, pp. 160–76.

13. Robert Doran, "Psychic conversion," *The Thomist* 41 (1977), 200–36; "Aesthetic subjectivity and generalized empirical method," *The Thomist* 43 (1979), 257–78.

14. Doran, p. 222.

15. Clifford Geertz, "Ethos, world view, and the analysis of sacred symbols," in *The Interpretation of Symbols* (New York: Basic Books, 1973), p. 127.

16. Langdon Gilkey, *Society and the Sacred* (New York: Crossroad, 1981), p. 60; "Organized 'religions' have traditionally provided that symbolic structure, orienting communal life in time to some permanent order and meaning. In a secular world, so-called ideologies, for example, liberal progressivism and Marxism, have done the same thing."

17. Rudolf Otto, *The Idea of the Holy: An Inquiry into the Non-Rational in an Idea of the Divine and Its Relation to the Rational,* trans. from the 9th German ed. by J. Harvey (London: Penguin, 1959).

18. Raimondo Panikkar, "La foi dimension constitutive de l'homme," *Archivio di Filosofia* 36 (1966), 17–28.

19. Paul Ricoeur, "Manifestation et proclamation," *Archivio di Filosofia* 44 (1974), 57–76.

20. David Tracy, *Blessed Rage for Order: The New Pluralism in Theology* (New York: Seabury Press, 1975), pp. 91–118.

21. Matthew Lamb, *Solidarity with Victims: Towards a Theology of Social Transformation* (New York: Crossroad, 1982), pp. 1–27; J. B. Metz, *Faith in History and Society:*

Toward a Practical Fundamental Theology (New York: Seabury, 1980), pp. 88–135.

22. Hans Urs Von Balthasar, *Love Alone* (New York: Herder & Herder, 1969), pp. 42–43.

23. Louis Bouyer, *Rite and Man: Natural Sacredness and Christian Liturgy* (Notre Dame, Ind.: University of Notre Dame Press, 1963).

24. Louis Bouyer, *Le Père Invisible* (Paris: Cerf, 1976).

25. Bernard Lonergan, however, associates this with an undifferentiated stage of meaning; *Method in Theology* (New York: Herder & Herder, 1972), p. 108.

Chapter Four

Ritual and Verbal Image

Some recent philosophers stress the linguisticality of understanding and reality.[1] Being stands forth in language, and it is only through language that we participate in Being. There is no access to knowledge of things, just as there is no access to self-knowledge, except through language. While language serves discursive, practical, and theoretical purposes, its primary nature is symbolic or presentational. It represents things in their relationships to one another. This is why ordinary, every-day language, what we use in naming things and in the predications we make of them, already offers insight into the poetic nature of human dwelling. Simple words—jug, water, wine, bread—hold together earth and sky, times past and times future, humanity's boundedness to earth and its desire for a fulfillment that breaks this boundedness. The full achievement of language can be found in the arts, but their accomplishment rests on the power of ordinary words, on the way that language possesses the human person rather than being an instrument in one's mouth or hand. Writers such as James Joyce and John Synge, in their seeming indulgence in verbal sounds, are exploring the resonances and possibilities of signification in the most simple and commonplace of words, while also showing a fascination with the ever-present possibility of new words, coming forth with new revelations.

Although this power of language is to be kept in mind, its relation to the bodily must be explored. The symbolic has been described already as the transformation of experience and the bringing of experience to formal expression so that it may be understood and given new projection, with new virtual possibilities of being and action. In fact, ordinary words are not the most rudimentary expressions of experience, even if they do serve in a culture as a key to its interpretation. Experience has a structure that is prior to linguisticality, one that can be investigated through reference to play and ritual.[2]

RITUAL

In the body and through the body, human persons find and express themselves in relation to environment, to other persons, to society, and to history. In and through the body they have the initial experiences associated with the sacred, experiences formulated interpretatively in some bodily ritual. Before any of these relationships are brought to language, they are given in some rudimentary form through bodily experience. The initial appropriation of relations to others and to self is in bodily reaction, gesture, and disposition. "Initial" does not have simply a chronological sense—attempts to write the prehistory of human expression have little success—but indicates that throughout life and in all forms of social interaction the bodily remains the fundamental mode whereby experience is received and given structure and articulation.

In his book *Homo Ludens,* Johan Huizinga explored the relationship between play and ritual, and for some years this relationship was the topic of several works.[3] Play expresses a perception of body and cosmos and is an instinctive form of self-expression and interaction that is unreflected, undistanced, and therefore not interested in presenting intelligible form. Play moves quickly to the point of *game,* however, where rules and patterns are decided, so that play takes place within the compass and according to the patterns determined. One can see children engaged in wild and exuberant play, but soon enough some toddler emerges to set rules, assign parts, and demand repetition. As such, a game is not for spectators, but tries and tests players and allows them to play out structures of being and, in playing, to appropriate them. When a game is played before an audience, the trend is to engage the audience in it.

Ritual provides a greater degree of abstraction than does a game, since its rules, rhythms, and repetitions are more definite and demand a more exact observance. Historical, anthropological, and sociological investigations point to ritual as formalized play. It marks the key moments of seasons and life, it manages order and chaos in times of change, and it is one of the necessities of social ordering and behavior. Sometimes what is called "primitive" ritual is associated with magic, since observers think that the intention of such ritual is to influence the powers that control life. This is not exact, however, for ritual is more an expression of harmony with, perception into, and conformity with the patterns of bios and cosmos.[4] Like a game, ritual is not done for spectators. In this it is distinguished from the arts, where the presentation of forms of meaning to an audience is integral to a work. Art is more concerned with fresh articulation and explores virtual meaning and new insight, whereas ritual expresses socially accepted patterns and harmonies, and the depth of its insight is less than in language and art.

Perhaps the contrast between ritual and art should not be made too sharply. This is especially so if language in ritual is considered, but it is so even when we consider only the bodily, whether this be the more complex form of dance or simple actions such as posture and table sharing. First, ritual is not only for the performers in the immediate moment of its enactment. As part of a cultural or social tradition, it has a place in the life of the group other than that of its being performed. It must be perceived precisely as an expression of a tradition. To this extent, ritual requires its cultural adherents to distance themselves from it and to appropriate it in ways comparable to the appropriation of written texts or artifacts. A good understanding of ritual's place in a group's life would be to say that its full meaning is perceived only in reflection subsequent to its performance.[5] Otherwise, participants remain only with undifferentiated feelings of order, harmony, grace, resolution of conflict, and the like that are experienced in its performance, but never enter by inner personal conversion into what it signifies.

A second point on which the contrast between works of art and ritual must be nuanced concerns the fixity or traditional nature of ritual, as opposed to the creative force of art. While it is true that ritual is concerned with traditional insight and meaning, so that familiarity and repetition are necessary, this ought not to blind us to the exploration of new meaning possible in ritual. One area of study that captures the minds of scholars is the nature of ritual change and its relation to social and cultural change. They occur in tandem, but the nature of the dialectic is hard to explain.[6] It does not seem the case that new ritual is elaborated simply to express the new social meaning and order. Rather, ritual's capacity to encompass explorations of fresh insight, even in bodily movement, gives it a place among the factors of social and cultural change or common meaning. A good example of this, taken from liturgy, is the relative importance given to consecration and communion in the eucharist. The understanding of church and the Christian mystery differs significantly according to whether the eucharistic climax is experienced at the elevation of the species or at the shared table. Setting aside historical reflection on why there was a shift from communion to elevation,[7] the shift in contemporary practice, which gives importance to the shared bread and cup, not only results from a new theology but actually gives a fresh understanding of the church's nature. Nor does this result simply from behavioristic manipulation by scribes. Rather it is an experiment in which communities engage and whose possibilities are within the traditional form of the eucharistic ritual as handed down to this time. Later on it will be necessary to discuss the role of the word in this kind of ritual insight.

One school of the history of religions, that associated most particularly with Mircea Eliade,[8] exhibits a primary interest in the bodily ritual that relates body and cosmos. Cosmic rituals—which celebrate the manifestation of the holy or the divine in the movements of night and day and in the flow of the seasons, or which commemorate hierophanies in sacred places or the presence of sacred power in such things as trees and rivers—bind humanity's destiny with respect for nature, a sense of awe before it, and a necessary oneness with it and with the powers that control it. When this sense of harmony and awe, which is expressed in bodily rites and attitudes, vanishes as it has in contemporary Western society (as recalled in the analysis of crisis presented by Gibson Winter), then conflicts, chaos, and exploitation ensue. Some look to ritual to revive these sentiments. Behind the interest in cosmic rites and symbols sometimes lies the persuasion that the divine, even in Judeo-Christian religion, is manifested in this form of revelation. This will be taken up again when we speak about myth and the relation between rite and myth. Suffice to say for now that the kind of investigation of religions associated with Eliade, and before him with Rudolf Otto, sees religion, with its rituals and symbols, as expressing the experience of the sacred given in cosmic hierophany. This approach takes on a more sophisticated or philosophical form in those contemporary theologians who write of limit-experiences, relating to body and cosmos, not precisely as experiences of the sacred but as experiences which, being "signals of the transcendent," create the space wherein to be sensitive to the religious message.

Another approach to the bodily element in ritual looks to studies that analyze religious symbol in virtue of a set of basic bodily experiences, taking these as cues to the entire range of the human.[9] These experiences are presented as the basis for ritual action and symbolic imagination. Thus three acts—remote action, copulation, and digestion—become reference points for understanding the symbolic and, more particularly, a range of symbolic actions. Ritual action does not use these actions in their normal rendering, but imitates them in a variety of ways, such as to present their meaningfulness and the meaningfulness of actions referable to them. In that sense, their imitation presents what the philosophers would call the structure of human experience before it is brought to language.[10]

In remote action, one acts toward persons or things in virtue of a separate and distinct personal identity. This includes actions such as moving away from, looking at, listening to, and touching. Whether the ritual actions derived from this type of bodily expression signify individuation or alienation, it is bodily or personal individuality that is signified. Except in cases of ritual sex, copulation is not a ritual action, but it does serve as the analogue for a second group of rites which somehow imitate this fundamental human experience of sexual union. Such rites are initiation ceremonies, sacrifice in certain of its features, and sacred dance as interacted rhythm, all of which carry a meaning of bonding persons together, or bonding persons with things and otherly realities, even while keeping their separateness intact. The third basic bodily function, digestion, provides the analogue for rituals that signify intimacy and mystical union. What is signified is fusion, two becoming one, where distinction is not felt or attended to, as when food is assimilated into the stomach. Although copulation is sometimes used as an image in mystical language, this is simply due to cultural traditions that assimilate it to the digestive in order to express the union to which sexual union aspires rather than that which it attains. After copulation, people are again apart, even though they feel bound to one another. Digestion is experienced as a more complete assimilation (although it is an image which allows for an ironic twist, as when James Joyce associates it with defecation).

Even when a classification of this sort is adopted as an avenue of insight into the shaping of experience by ritual, it must be remembered that rites and their signification interplay with one another. Some rites carry patterns of two or more of these categories. For example, the ordering of a ritual meal, with its allotment of roles and places, indicates separation and distinction, but it is also a binding action of covenant and a symbol of communion as one body. Baptismal immersion is an assimilation of personal identity and a journey (ascending from the pool), as it is an action of initiation into a covenant group and a fusion of identities expressed in the images of descent into the earth or return to the womb. Most important to remember from this classification is that ritual represents and imitates the most fundamental bodily experiences, which are separate identity, coming together in mutual bond, and fusing identities to the point of blurred distinctions.

SOME PARTICULAR RITUALS

Three types of religious ritual that relate to the cosmic and the bodily have received special attention and are increasingly invoked as paradigms for understanding Christian liturgy. The value of this insight and the nuances with which it is to be accepted are worth attention. These three types of ritual are rites of taboo and purification, rites of passage, and mimetic rites.

Rites of Purification and Taboo
The establishment of taboos, and the purification rites made necessary by their infringement, is a basic way for a society to mark out the field of the sacred and designate the vital forces and powers that it feels the need to identify with and serve in ordering its life and projecting its vision of reality.[11] Today people are often horrified when they hear of the old Catholic practices of a mother's purification after childbirth or penances imposed on spouses who received communion the morning after having sexual relations. Taboo is an odious word to modern ears, and the practices mentioned may be deemed to reflect both superstition and sexual guilt or disdain. Today people may be less censorious, but still benignly amused, when they are told of the rigorous silence that once had to be kept in places of worship. Talking in church has since become a sign of liberation, and approaching communion after a night of extramarital sexual enjoyment is seen almost as a compliment to God.

It can hardly be questioned that superstition, misplaced guilt, and ecclesiastical efforts to dominate people by controlling their intimate lives had something to do with these and similar rituals. It would be a mistake, however, to see this as their main source and reason. A woman's seclusion from social contact after childbirth, practiced in so many societies, did not express a sense of wrongdoing or of guilt in sex and childbearing. Rather, it expressed awe and fear in face of the life-force or sacred power with which one is united in sex and in giving life. One contracts impurity by showing disregard for this, and one who has been in touch with the sacred must undergo rites of purification before others dare to resume contact with that person. A mother and her newborn were deemed to be in a sacred space which others dare not approach. The mother and child had to reenter the realm of the profane before others could resume normal relations with them.

All rites of taboo and purification have a similar character. They may be outmoded and impatient of use today, but the sense of things expressed in them needs to be integrated in some new way into our vision of reality. Turning the "churching" of mothers into a prayer of thanksgiving is not adequate, unless the rite expresses awe in the face of new life and the generative force which is intrinsic to the woman-man relationship. Demythologization (and in this case depatriarchalization) must be a part of appropriating the meaning of such traditional rites, but appropriation in some form is necessary to the bodily and cosmic roots of the psyche and of the sense of the holy.

Rites of Passage
Rites of passage, the second type of religious ritual, owe their most significant study and classification to the work of Arnold Van Gennep.[12] Such rites are of three kinds: those which deal with the passage of the seasons and its significance for a human community; those which assist individuals and groups to move through the great passages of human life, namely, birth, adolescence, marriage, and death; and those which affect the passages or movements which must be faced by society as a whole, such as moving from one pasture to another for nomadic groups, the beginning and end of wars, or the transfer of ruling power. Van Gennep related all of these rites to socialization and discerned in all of them a common pattern. He divided the pattern into three stages: separation, liminality, and reentry or reintegration.

The pattern is exemplified most easily in the set of rites affecting an individual's change in social status and responsibility, whether through a life-passage or through induction into office. To move into the new position and encounter the holy powers which watch over and animate the society, the person must first be separated from the community in ceremonies which represent a cutting off from old relationships and renouncing former behavioral patterns. The person then spends a period of time in a stage of liminality or marginality, where he or she is forced to experience the core of the self and communion with others, as presented in the fundamental myths of the society and in ways which wipe away any trace of social status or dignity. Then by the final rites of reentry, the person returns to the community and assumes a new status and responsibility. It is interesting that in traditional societies, rites of passage are also performed for the dead since the dead are considered to remain members of the society, having a part to play in its life but in a new social position.

Sometimes this kind of anthropological paradigm is invoked by sacramental theologians. First, it serves as a useful model to explain the catechumenate, especially the catechumens' marginality, their learning of the beliefs and stories of the Christian community, and the final aggregation to the community in the sacraments of the paschal night. In a similar way, it serves as a model for other cases where a public transition takes place, such as in the canonical penance of the ancient church or in the preparation for, and ordination to, church office. Second, it serves as a model for the sevenfold sacramental system inasmuch as this is linked with the life-cycle, though in this case the usefulness of the model in offering any real insight is questionable.[13]

Mimetic Rites
The third category of rites mentioned is mimetic rites. This category overlaps with the previous two. The

designation *mimetic* comes from the nature of these rites as an imitation or representation of something else, for example, the story of the gods, the fundamental myths of the society, or cosmic and life-cycle rhythms. Naturally enough, the parallel with Christian liturgy rests on the idea that Christian sacrament is an imitation or representation of the mysteries of Christ.

Several remarks need to be made about comparisons of Christian liturgy with any of these rites. First, while Christian liturgy has shown a historical proclivity to adopt some of the patterns apparent in these rituals, the church has never been at ease with the tendency. Current studies on popular religion in the history of Christianity talk about the religion of the four seasons, meaning the four seasons of the year and the four seasons of human life, (birth, adolescence, marriage, and death). Without a doubt, history shows the church coming to terms with the felt need to mark these points of life, so that sacraments are attached to seasons of life and feasts to seasons of the year. The controversies over the relation of baptism to birth, over the link between confirmation and growing up, and over the concurrence between valid marriage and sacramental marriage are well known in both historical and pastoral theology. The attachment of Christmas to the winter solstice, the celebration of ember days, the importance attached in many places to the feasts of John the Baptist, the Annunciation, and the Assumption are historical facts and represent an ecclesiastical compromise with natural religious instincts. Whatever the links officially established or tolerated, it must be remembered that Christian liturgy is a celebration of historical event and personal conversion through grace and faith, so that intrinsically its rites bear no relation to the cycles of season and life, except inasmuch as they adopt some of their symbolism.[14] Indeed, there is an experience of power represented in cosmic and bodily symbolism, and Christian liturgy adverts to this in the interests of wholeness. Yet, what it celebrates is divine freedom and gratuity and the grace that comes to humanity thereby, prevailing over all contrary forces.

This brings us to the second observation, which affirms the immense difference between the historical religion and rites of Judaism and Christianity, on the one hand, and cosmic religion and its rites, on the other. The place of bodily ritual—with its evocation of deep human experience, its relations to cosmos and body and the unconscious—in Jewish and Christian worship can be understood only in the turn to the word, the commemoration of historical events in which God is revealed, and the antiritual bias, all of which are intrinsic and vital to the development of this form of worship.[15] The encounter with power and with vital forces that is expressed in the rites recalled briefly from the history of religions is not denied, but is integrated into a faith that celebrates God's free and gracious entry into human history. This means a move from images of the divine that are primarily cosmic or heroic to those expressive of love's gratuity, images joined to the promises of liberation that emerge from the events of divine intervention in history. In other words, what is expressed is God's "nonidentity" with what is symbolized in the cosmic and in the bodily manifestations of the sacred. The Jewish and Christian people are promised freedom in the face of the powers thus manifested, not a freedom that ignores humanity's need for harmony with the bodily and the cosmic, but one that with confidence in God's Spirit allows them a creative rather than a servile participation in the building of humanity's future.

Images of cosmos and body, representative of the power and life that they reveal and of the initial structuring of human experience, do carry over into liturgy. In that sense they offer intuition of a structure which needs to be integrated into personal and social experience. The images and symbols are a constant reminder of finitude, of the forces to be integrated, and of the risk of either flouting these forces or becoming enslaved to them. The graciousness of God promises a liberation that cannot come from cosmic religion, however, and this is what is symbolized and celebrated.

This leads to a further remark touching particularly on life-passage and liturgy. There should be no confusion, even if there is a connection, between the socialization process and conversion to Christ affirmed in sacrament. Sacramental theology and pastoral practice suffer when the connection is pushed, even granting some usefulness in the images of passage and its stages in explaining liturgical process. Baptism, the primary sacrament of Christian faith and conversion, knows nothing about a specific age or the community's social expectations of persons of certain ages. The church is a free community, and conversion to Christ is not a matter of age but of grace and personal engagement. The many current controversies about confirmation illustrate how a discussion is befuddled when the question of age enters.[16] There are serious discussions about the advisability of making valid marriage and Christian marriage coincide.[17] When in European society Christianity was the dominant religion, and a religious sense pervaded the culture and social ordering, it was almost inevitable that the church's liturgy would be adapted to the socialization process affecting good citizens and one's place in the social order. Today, the nature of Christian faith and community would stand out more clearly if all temporal relations with the socialization process affecting membership in secular society were cut.

A final remark on this evocation of cosmic and bodily ritual concerns the kind of ritual most prominent in Christian liturgy. Christian ritual is somewhat parabolic, so that it constitutes a disclosure of divine presence very different from cosmic religion. In fact, though cosmic images are found in Christian liturgical symbolism (Easter abounds in them), its rituals do not of their nature evoke either seasonal or human cycles. The bodily things that Christian liturgy incorporates are more ordinary, more daily, more domestic. They are the life of every day, not the drama or heroism of wrestling with the chaos of passage. The things used are simple: bread, wine, water, and oil. The actions are homely, nurturing, and caring, such as breaking bread, pouring wine, bathing, touching, and salving with oil. Inasmuch as liturgy has been associated with more social purposes and has taken on all the burden of religious desire in civic society, it has absorbed more of the cyclic. Yet, the parabolic and prophetic qualities of its core symbols demand to be eventually freed from all such associations. These very simple items and actions are to be held in great awe and respect for what they reveal by their nature. They lose their meaning in the liturgy when they are instrumentalized, either as means of grace, expressions of an institutionally bound notion of the divine, or as a means of establishing community order, such as happens when the cup is not freely given to all participants in the eucharist. Bread and wine or the touch of a hand, in their very simplicity, hold together "earth, sky, gods, and mortals."[18] They point more to the daily and domestic, rather than to the extraordinary, as the place where being and human dwelling show forth, where things and humanity together come to be. As the focus of the hermeneutic of traditional texts is on everyday language as the key to understanding, so the focus of sacramental understanding is on these daily and domestic things.

The bodily element is indeed essential to Christian worship, for Christians do not celebrate some pseudo-mystical cult, and many of the images of cosmic religion are retained in it. Bodily actions and cosmic images are incorporated in such a way, however, that they refer to fellowship in Jesus Christ rather than to participation in a mythical reality or in cosmic rhythms. As practiced in a variety of religions, a meal has certainly acquired many cultic connotations as sacrifice and godly feast, but the eating and drinking that are the heart of the Christian eucharist are modest and sober, taking their meaning from domestic meals rather than from cultic meals. Indeed, the New Testament literature does not use cultic language for the church's acts of worship, but transfers this kind of language to the people themselves or to the death of Christ. It is in holiness, obedience, and willing testimony to God's love, and in the hope rooted in this, that all worship is fulfilled and thus changed radically. The eucharist is a celebration and an act of worship because of the people who celebrate it in faith. If those participating do not live the gospel fellowship in earnest, their act is more a profanation than a proclamation of the Lord's death.

Similar remarks could be made about water immersion. This rite was not invented by early Christians, but was adopted by them as a rite of entry into the community. However, the reference to the cross of Christ and to faith in him determined its meaning. It is then an act of incorporation by faith into Jesus' death rather than a rite of ritual purification or mythical initiation.

That this "antiritual" type of celebration should constitute the core of Christian worship is significant for what it says about the Christian's relation to society. A close relationship exists between how people perform in the body and how they relate to the social body. Sociologists study religious cults in terms of what they say about the sect's relation to society.[19] In this century, a greater distinction must be made between acts of Christian worship and those rituals, formal or informal, whereby members of the churches effect their relations to the body social and politic. Normally, socialization is the same for Christians as for others, insofar as they accept society's outlook on reality and its values. In their own worship, they express what type of community or fellowship they are among themselves, as well as the values to which they contribute by reason of their faith in Christ. This can actually give them a certain freedom in the face of social and cultural pressures. The bodily mode of Christian worship, as it has been described here, and not only the verbal, can enhance the prophetic role that a Christian community plays in society.

VERBAL IMAGES: THE FIRST MOVE TO LANGUAGE[20]
Since by now it is quite clear that the place of the bodily and the cosmic in Christian liturgy is bound up with word, and changed by word, it is time to turn to the transformation of experience when it is brought to speech. Bodily ritual, besides being the "played out" insight into patterns of experience, is also the source of visual and other sensory images. In the turn to language, verbal images carry insight into experience a stage further and are free to integrate the insights of body into new perspectives.

One can make six propositions about the place of the verbal symbol in the articulation of human experience, the last two of which will require further explanation:

1. It is language at its most dense, or thickest, taking hold of reality in ways not reducible to conceptual abstraction, whatever openings it gives to philosophical thought.

2. It points back to its basis in that which is not yet language.

3. Its polysemy, which leaves it open to several meanings and to be used in reference to different things, remains even when its meaning is determined by context, and this affects the evocative power of its usage.

4. It describes limit-situations in human experience and existence that are not totally available to philosophic thought.

5. Its meaning is determined within myth, or story, where it is connected with other images or symbols, so that there is an interplay between them and an integration of insights into multilayered experience through a progression of images.

6. Symbolic language is the only access to dealing with certain experiences, such as evil, since they are not available for philosophical thought and reasoned explanation by reason of their negative nature.

An explanation of the last proposition will come more suitably after a discussion of myth, so that at this juncture the fifth proposition will receive attention, isolating reference to verbal images from the context of myth. This proposition can be explained best by referring to Paul Ricoeur's explanation of the images of stain, sin, and guilt in the Judeo-Christian tradition, followed by some reflections on how similar interlacing of images occurs in liturgical language.

The first, most undifferentiated, and most external experience of evil is expressed in images that cluster around that of *stain*. They are material images and connote a feeling of infection by something outside the person. At this level of experience, a close affinity exists between the cosmic and the biological, for what is brought to language is the person's feeling of alienation and of being blemished, so that the need for rites of purification may be strong. The ethical implications of stain are not clear.

The image of *sin*, and others that go along with it, such as wandering, exile, and desert, no longer represent evil as something of the external and material order. Sin is done by human persons and affects relations with a personal sacred. In the Old Testament, this kind of imagery belongs within the context of the alliance between God and the people of Israel. The sense of blemish or stain, of something external to the person and the community, is not discarded totally. Rather, the image of stain is integrated into that of sin, so that while evil is symbolized as something done by human persons, it still seems to have an origin outside the human community in the material world. In this sense, before human persons stray and sin, evil is already there.

The symbol of *guilt* represents a further interiorization of evil and of responsibility for it. Sins do not belong simply to the human person as something internal, a source of a broken relationship with God, but now they appear as actions for which one has to answer before God. The sense of accountability, of the need to take stock of one's fault and of its consequences, is added to the interiority already present in the image of sin.

In these examples of symbols of evil, there is a progression in which one set of images builds on another, so that through their interplay a comprehensive and total representation of the experience of evil is presented, an experience which is as it were multilayered. In the progression from one level to the next, the first stage is not abandoned. It is broken with initially, but then is taken up again and integrated for what it expresses of truth in the higher perspective. Images of evil, however intense their significance of personal responsibility, continue to include the representation of evil as a given that somehow precedes human action, just as they represent alienation from one's own body and from the cosmos, as well as from God. Similarly, the images of the tribunal which underscore personal responsibility integrate those of a broken relationship with the one before whom one stands guilty, as well as the sense of incapacity contained in images of captivity, wandering, and exile. For this reason, it becomes clear that merely answering before a tribunal does not bring deliverance from sin, but a redemptive intervention on the part of the accuser is required.

As a summary of this threefold symbolism of evil expressed in images—which of course reveal their full meaning only in the context of story—we can say that first there is the articulation of the external element, then that of the interpersonal, and third that of personal responsibility. None of the images can be discarded if evil is to be expressed adequately and so faced in its totality. Only when rationalization leads to a disregard for the first two levels of expression, thus focusing almost entirely on personal responsibility, does religion degenerate into legalism, which then includes much that is but a sublimation of the impurity and purification stage of religious expression. The severe bodily penances of an early stage in medieval penitential practice may have been spelled out in terms of satisfaction and computed carefully as reparation, but their very severity may indicate revenge worked upon the body in a kind of sublimated purification.

Corresponding to the threefold symbolism of evil is a threefold symbolism of redemption. First is the symbolism of purification, to deal with infection and the element of exteriority in evil. Second is the symbolism of bringing back, of redeeming, of healing the broken covenant. Third is the symbolism of expiation, but precisely because guilt has to include sin and stain, so expiation cannot be made by the sinner but has to be vicarious, done not by oneself but given to one in grace. Expiation for sin cannot be represented simply as "measure for measure." Even in acknowledging fault, the person and the race face the impossibility of repairing justice, of mending broken relationships, of overcoming the evil present in the world. To this the gospel proclaims the divine response: "Where sin abounded, grace does more abound."

Liturgical symbolism incorporates in one way or another this thrice-interpreted experience of evil and desire for redemption. Some liturgical symbols are at the level of the material and exteriority, as when liturgy includes taboos and rites of purification, or at least images retained from these. The image or the word conjoined to the action is what we are interested in, however, so it is of interest to see how an external action may be accompanied by images of all three kinds. Water immersion, or the sprinkling with water that begins a Sunday service, is spoken of in the first place as purification from stain, or as washing in the blood of Christ. Evoking the image of the waters of the Red Sea or the Jordan adds images of release from exile and captivity. The confession of fault and faith incorporates the element of personal responsibility.

Of course, images do not remain semantically pure, expressing always or uniquely what their lexical meaning signifies. They gain weight, extension, and thickness by their continued use and from the contexts in which they occur. This is not meant to discredit looking for "the second meaning given in the first," but simply points out that a word or image resonates with its use and in context can carry an accumulation of many images. Thus the word *sin,* for all its original meaning of straying, conjures up all that is likewise signified in the images of stain and guilt.

This is also true for such a central liturgical symbol as sacrifice, which is predicated of Christ's death, of the Christian people, of their deeds, and of the Lord's Supper.[21] The multiple reference it has picked up is already a warning of cumulative imagery and significance, or of a condensation of meanings. Dealing with a word image that harks back to a rather ambiguous ritual practice complicates interpretation. Whatever is said about such complications, of itself sacrifice is an image which belongs at the first level of articulated experience, that of the material and exteriority. It expresses the need for reconciliation with cosmic forces, for purification, for setting things aside and making them holy, thus delimiting the space of the holy and the actions pertaining to it. As practiced by Israel, sacrifice was more interiorized, as in mercy offerings where it signified the gratuity of God's forgiveness in the face of human straying. But sacrifices were also made in contexts of reparation and expiation for fault; thus, added to the original significance of exteriority were those of progressive interiority. It is at this stage of accumulated significance that it is employed metaphorically in the Christian context. Retention of three kinds of imagery is the key to interpreting Christian sacrifice, for example when it is used to interpret Christ's death. In this case the foremost meaning is taken sometimes to be that of expiation or reparation. Only if we realize that it carries the meaning of God's gratuitous mercy, however, can we understand properly what is meant by calling it an act of vicarious, rather than representative, expiation. In other words, Jesus Christ makes expiation not because he legally represents the human race, but because in solidarity with the race his action is one of gratuitous self-giving, issuing from God's merciful love. Thus as an image of interpretation that touches on all three levels of the experience of evil, sacrifice represents Christ's death as that act whereby (1) humanity is reconciled with the material world and cleansed of the infection of sin, (2) God's gracious initiative and forgiveness answers humanity's need, and (3) expiation comes nonetheless through an act done within the race in human solidarity by one who stands in the most intimate relationship with God.

Whatever belongs within human experience when it is addressed in liturgy is touched at this threefold level and in imagery representative of it. All human experience is marred by sin; all human experience is redeemed in Christ. As the old axiom had it, what is not assumed is not redeemed. This may be exemplified by the way that marriage is spoken of when celebrated in liturgy. Marriage is experienced first at the physical level, as a union in the flesh and as an encounter with vital forces and sacred powers. It is also at this level that it is first blemished by sin, so that disharmony, sexual taboos, and pain in childbearing become physical images of tainted marriage. Marriage is also represented as a covenant relationship, a union between persons who bond themselves to one another and in this bonding to society. At this level marriage suffers when the covenant with God is broken and the interests of a deviant people prevail over the interests of marriage, as for example in the patriarchalization of marriage customs and relations. Despite this, marriage as covenant remains a wondrous image of divine love and is represented as something which can be healed by the very love which it signifies. In marriage ceremonies, the union is also represented in images such as that of contract, and thus as a union in which partners acknowledge responsibility to one another and to society. Yet here too it is open to fault in forms such as adultery. In marriage liturgy we find accumulated and rather jumbled symbols of two in one flesh, painful childbirth, and shame in nudity, symbols of fidelity and infidelity, and symbols of contract and violation of rights. Because the experience is evoked so totally, it is possible by a kind of second naiveté to celebrate marriage as both a healing and a joy at all three levels of its symbolization. When the interpretation is not made and reflected upon, we run the risk of allowing certain images to prevail and thus of distorting marriage.

CONCLUSION
In this chapter, we discussed how ritual and verbal images constitute elements of the Christian symbol. In talking of ritual, it was necessary to make clear

104

distinctions between the ritual of hierophany and the
Christian ritual, since the meaning and significance of
rite in Christianity is much affected by the domination
of word over rite. Many images associated with cosmic
ritual still have significance in Christian liturgy, but this
is so in the way these images are brought into a new
context. The holy is not where cosmic ritual looks for it,
but in places distinctive of a historical revelation. This
discussion allowed us to clarify how liturgy takes up
the shaping of experience that occurs in the body prior
to the speaking of any word. We then went on to
discuss verbal images, the first move to language. We
saw how these develop and progress in revelation but
continue to make it possible in worship to express the
many different levels of human experience by absorbing
one level into the next. In the next chapter, we will
examine these images in the context of myth.

NOTES

1. Hans-Georg Gadamer, "Man and language" and "The
nature of things and the language of things," in *Philosophical
Hermeneutics* (Berkeley: University of California Press, 1977),
pp. 59–68, 69–81; Paul Ricoeur, "A philosophical journey.
From existentialism to the philosophy of language,"
Philosophy Today 17 (1973), 88–96.

2. Hans-Georg Gadamer, *Truth and Method* (New York:
Crossroad, 1982), pp. 94–105; Johan Huizinga, *Homo Ludens.
A Study of the Play-Element in Culture* (Boston: Beacon Press,
1955); Gibson Winter, *Liberating Creation: Foundations of Social
Ethics* (New York: Crossroad, 1981), pp. 10–19.

3. For example, Harvey Cox, *The Feast of Fools* (Cambridge,
Mass.: Harvard University Press, 1969).

4. Susanne K. Langer, *Philosophy in a New Key: A Study in the
Symbolism of Reason, Rite, and Art,* 3rd ed. (Cambridge, Mass.:
Harvard University Press, 1978), pp. 144–70.

5. Such a traditional practice as mystagogical catechesis, or
such a traditional theory as the permanence of baptism

because of the word invoked, are consonant with this way of seeing ritual's role.

6. There is a brief survey of the question in George S. Worgul, *From Magic to Metaphor: A Validation of the Christian Sacraments* (New York: Paulist Press, 1980), pp. 94–105.

7. Nathan Mitchell, *Cult and Controversy: The Worship of the Eucharist Outside Mass* (New York: Pueblo, 1982).

8. Mircea Eliade is at present engaged in writing a history of religious ideas. Two volumes have appeared: *A History of Religious Ideas,* translated by Willard R. Trask, 2 vols. (Chicago: University of Chicago Press, 1978, 1981).

9. Gilbert Durand, *Les Structures Anthropologiques de l'Imaginaire. Introduction à l'Archétypologie Général* (Paris: Bordas, 1969); *L'Imagination Symbolique* (Paris: Presses Universitaires, 1968); B. R. Brinkman, "On sacramental man," *The Heythrop Journal* 13 (1972), 371–401; 14 (1973), 5–39, 162–89, 280–306, 396–416.

10. Paul Ricoeur, "Metaphor and symbol," *Interpretation Theory: Discourse and the Surplus of Meaning* (Fort Worth: Texas Christian University Press, 1976), pp. 60–65.

11. Mary Douglas, *Purity and Danger: An Analysis of Concepts of Pollution and Taboo* (London: Routledge & Kegan Paul, 1966).

12. Arnold Van Gennep, *The Rites of Passage* (Chicago: University of Chicago Press, 1960). See Luis Maldonado & David Power (eds.), *Liturgy and Human Passage, Concilium* 112 (New York: Seabury Press, 1979).

13. David Power, "The odyssey of man in Christ," *Concilium* 112, pp. 100–11.

14. Anscar Chupungco, *The Cosmic Elements of Christian Passover* (Rome: San Anselmo, 1977); "Liturgical feasts and the seasons of the year," *Concilium* 142 (New York: Seabury Press, 1981), 31–36.

15. Louis-Marie Chauvet, "La ritualité Chrétienne dans le cercle infernal du symbole," *La Maison-Dieu* 133:1 (1978), 31–77.

16. Günter Biemer, "Controversy on the age of confirmation as a typical example of conflict between the criteria of theology and the demands of pastoral practice," *Concilium* 112 (New York: Seabury Press, 1979), pp. 115–25.

17. Edward J. Kilmartin, "When is marriage a sacrament?" *Theological Studies* 34 (1973), 275–86.

18. The expression is taken from Martin Heidegger, "The thing," in *Poetry, Language and Thought* (New York: Harper & Row, 1975), p. 173.

19. Roger Bastide, *The African Religions of Brazil: Towards a Sociology of the Interpretation of Civilizations* (Baltimore: Johns Hopkins University Press, 1978); Mary Douglas, *Natural Symbols: Explorations in Cosmology* (New York: Pantheon, 1970), pp. 65–81.

20. What follows depends on Paul Ricoeur, *The Symbolism of Evil* (Boston: Beacon Press, 1967), and Beatriz Melano Couch, "Religious symbols and philosophical reflection," in Charles E. Reagan (ed.), *Studies in the Philosophy of Paul Ricoeur* (Athens: Ohio University Press, 1979), pp. 115–31.

21. Robert J. Daly, *Christian Sacrifice: The Judaeo-Christian Background before Origen* (Washington, D.C.: Catholic University of America Press, 1978); Frances M. Young, *Sacrifice and the Death of Christ* (Philadelphia: Fortress Press, 1975).

Chapter Five

Myth, Narrative, Metaphor

Symbols give determined meaning within the context of myth. The term "myth" is as slippery as symbol and is just as liable to be used in different ways, both orally and in writing. A twofold difficulty (of a nontechnical nature) is encountered in using the word. First, some immediately associate it with antiquity and with fabulous stories of gods and superhuman powers, so that its use today is immediately discountenanced. Second, for others myth means what is false, illusory, or merely fanciful, as when one says that to promise prosperity to all is pure myth. These difficulties aside, even in philosophical, anthropological, and literary writings we cannot find a single common approach. With reference to Christianity, and Christian liturgy in particular, two distinct questions must be considered. One is the place of the Adamic myth—which has no pretensions to being factually historical—in formulating beliefs and in providing a content to liturgical celebration. The other question concerns how the genus of myth may be employed to explain the narrative of historical events, particularly the Christ-event, and what light this sheds on liturgical commemoration.

Before approaching these two questions, let us begin with a general description of myth.[1] It is characteristic of myth that some profound truth is communicated in the form of a story. It interlaces many symbols and in the process unfolds new meaning because of the plot in the story. Myth is proclaimed to be the truth on which the ordinary world and immediate reality are based; it is the ultimate reality from which they derive their significance. Myth is cultural and social when it is commonly acknowledged among a people or peoples as pertinent to their life, their institutions, and their pursuits. Myth is more abstract in form than rite, as well as more complete. Whereas rite acknowledges the existence of hidden powers and vital forces, myth tells a story that explains the meaning of the world of these powers. The religious myth concerns ultimate meaning. Religious rite can refer back to the myth, and because of the appeal to the mysterious expressed in myth, can avoid descending into pure magic.

Since contemporary society is culturally pluriform, one can seldom speak of a modern society which has a commonly accepted religious myth. Furthermore, contemporary societies do not spell out their commonly accepted pattern of meanings and objectives in story form. Instead they look to laws and institutions to express their sense of reality. Hence, it is more often in antiquity or in primitive societies that one finds clear examples of the mythological. Nevertheless, in contemporary cultures there remain a number of underlying myths, or implicit myths, not formulated in ways which command explicit common consent, yet which are highly influential in the meanings they suggest and convey. Thus in the United States, President Reagan adopted the myth of the trek toward the west at his inauguration, and the combat between good and evil formerly represented in the western film is now carried on in "Star Wars." In Italy, a pantheon of heroes from the days of the unification of states is honored, and is added to gradually by tales of the resistance. In Ireland, the young are still fed on stories of Wolfe Tone and the Easter Rising, or conversely on those of the Battle of the Boyne and Edward Carson.

The determination of meaning within plot is apparent in the Adamic myth.[2] The images of stain, sin, and guilt, already examined in Chapter 4, occur within this story and yield their meaning within it. The temptation by the serpent takes up the image of stain, representing the sense of infection or of an evil that precedes the human act. Yet by reason of the plot, the story avoids attributing this evil either to God or to any other creative power. The banishment from paradise takes up the symbols of exile and broken covenant, representing sin as the loss of an intimate relationship with God that is intended for humanity and accessible to whoever is prepared to live by God's promises. Guilt is presented in the accusation to which Adam must respond. The story is completed not by the punishment meted out, but by the promise of redemption, so that the plot is not one of pure tragedy. Thus the myth expresses the experience of evil in the images of stain, sin, and guilt, and accepts the enigmatic character which these images articulate. Then it works this into a coherent narrative which allows for a meaningful response to evil where fault is acknowledged, a broken relationship lamented, and yet the perspective included that evil is not just the sum total of human wrongdoing but a power that infects humanity.

What is the place in Christian symbolism for such a myth, apparently without historical foundation? For many centuries it was taken by Christians to be factual, being invoked as the justification for child baptism, such that its telling easily produces a sense of disbelief, or even of disillusionment and privation. If it is not factually true, it is felt to reveal nothing of significance, or even to be misleading. Consequently, ideas about sin are thrown into disarray. One response is a straightforward demythologization where the story is translated into existential categories, with added appeal to the power of social evil. These categories then substitute for the story. Simply talking about human solidarity in sin does not have the same impact as telling a story about it, however, and can leave out what is carried over into the experience of evil from the cosmic or ritual patterning of experience.

The place of the Adamic myth in Christian symbolism, and its continuing pertinence to contemporary experience, is better understood if it is realized that a choice between fact and fancy is not at stake. The story is not that of a particular person inserted into some point of history, but is written more in terms of a universal history, that is, a story descriptive of a common and oft-repeated human experience in the face of evil which occurs at any period of history or in any historical situation. The enigma is ever the same. Evil and sin escape a clear historical account that marks an unmistakable beginning, the act that ushered it in. Evil and sin belong in history, yet their own history cannot be clearly told. Philosophically, the same tension between human responsibility and ontological basis occurs. On either score, humanity is left in a dilemma between protesting innocence and admitting guilt, between accepting responsibility and blaming God, between trying to overcome evil and knowing that without God it cannot be overcome. The Adamic story offers a pattern of response rather than an explanation, either historical or philosophical. It makes it possible to steer one's way between the apparent necessity of evil and the nonnecessity of bad moral choice, between evil's inevitable occurrence and its historical contingency. The story is a horizon of redemption given to be interiorized, not a solution to historical and philosophical enigmas. As explained by Paul Ricoeur, this redemptive horizon comes from the way in which the Adamic myth integrates three other types of myth by which human societies have endeavored to account for evil and set a pattern of human response to it. *Cosmogonic myth* settles the dilemma by attributing the source of evil neither to humanity nor to God but to

other creative powers or gods. The Adamic story rejects
this explanation, while in the person of the serpent it
accepts the ambiguity of evil's origins. The *myth of exile*
focuses on broken relationship and includes the sense
of exteriority present in the serpent by its image of a
lost paradise. The *classical tragic myth,* typified in the
Oedipus story, allows the hero to complain that the
incest and parricide which set him at odds with his
own parents were committed by him unknowingly and
unwittingly because of circumstances for which he was
not responsible. Yet, he acknowledges in the end that
the source of his sin was his own pride and anger. The
Adamic story includes the basic elements of all three
kinds of myth, but overcomes their dilemma by being
not an etiology but a story of expected redemption. The
anticipation of the end gives a new character to what is
presented for interiorization.[3]

The Bible and the liturgy continue to draw on the
Adamic myth and have often inflated the figure of the
serpent when evil is represented as lurking in such
personifications as Satan, demons, and principalities
and powers. It is this inflation which causes further
problems in contemporary liturgical renewal.
Representations of evil in the liturgy are often
historically and culturally conditioned images of the
particular type of evil that an age or a people
confronts. Representations in the Western liturgy seem
to have lost firm rooting in any kind of foundational
myth. One can see the liturgy running the gamut
between a schema of exteriority and a schema of
interiority, with the former all too often predominating,
particularly in the case of exorcisms. Looking to the
model of exorcism in the stories of Jesus casting out
demons, one notices how the image of subjection to an
external power, though retained, is secondary to the
faith and trust in Jesus that is demanded from the
person as a fitting response, or even as a condition. In
early liturgical books, there are exorcisms for such

things as the water and the oil to be used in the sacraments, but the euchology relates this both to the creation story and to the story of Jesus. In later texts, such as the tenth-century *Pontificale Romano-Germanicum,* demons are found everywhere, lurking in fields and granaries, in mills and in kitchens, and affecting people with dread and inexplicable diseases.[4] This is a gross externalization of evil powers and of the way to be released from them. It is the picture of a society which is prey to dark forces and goblin spirits, a society which always seems to rely on external signs, even when human truth is put to the test, as in the ceremony for testing the truth of a witness by placing one of the person's limbs in boiling water.

This vast tendency to people the world with demons and to attribute every ill, spiritual or physical, to them goes far beyond the Adamic myth with its figure of the serpent. Yet by reacting against too much personification of evil, the current language of the revised books uses clinically pure language that traces everything physical back to its source in the biologically ascertainable and everything moral to its source in the human conscience. The risk is to forswear the Adamic myth completely, to the omission of all that it signifies about the exteriority of evil and the tragic nature of human existence. If this happens, the community is left uncertain in the language of its address to God, since it lacks the symbolic language to represent the conflict in which it is caught. The language of the laboratory or the counselor's office fails to render the magnitude, the ambiguity, the enigma of evil and sin, or the extent to which humanity in darkness must turn to God for healing and forgiveness. Divine mercy is the horizon within which technical and moral battles are fought, not the divine justice represented when only the symbolism of guilt is kept. If everything must be explained with scientific clarity, or even in the commonsense terms of every day, people are placed in

113

the unending search for answers. Symbolic language, inclusive of image and story, describes more tellingly the orbit within which choices are made and reality interiorized, both the inevitable tragedy of evil and the responsibility for one's own actions, as well as the hope in which both can be faced and which becomes the wellspring of good actions.

This then is one kind of myth that continues to offer a basis to the sacramental system, inasmuch as sacraments celebrate redemption from evil and Christ's power over it. It has affinities with cosmological myth because it tells no particular history and is not to be taken as pseudo-history, but instead tells the story of humanity's tragic encounter with evil in universal terms. Unlike cosmogonies, however, it is not the story of the gods but of humanity itself, interpreting a common experience.

MYTH AND NARRATIVE: REMEMBERING EVENTS
It is relatively simple to see how mythical elements were woven into the narrative of the Old Testament events, or even into the story and then into the liturgical celebration of Jesus Christ. It is not so easy to say in what sense myth serves as liturgical paradigm for the relation of worship or sacrament to the death of Christ. Can liturgy be related to the story of Christ in ways similar to that in which rite is related to myth? Much seems to depend on whether one takes ancient religious myth as the point of comparison, or *mythos* as defined by some literary critics in the wake of Aristotle's use of the term.

The first approach was popularized in liturgical studies by the school of Maria Laach, and especially by Odo Casel in his theory of *Mysteriengegenwart.*[5] Perhaps it has even more lasting influence because of the work of Mircea Eliade. The second approach to myth is being assimilated into biblical studies, with a renewed interest in the Bible as literature, but it has received little attention in the field of liturgical theology. It is liable to give more importance to the place of narrative in liturgical celebration, however, and to establish the relation between narrative and keeping memory. This would be in keeping with Judeo-Christian worship's primacy of word over ritual.

Let us consider the first approach, particularly in the thought of Mircea Eliade and then in Louis Bouyer's reaction to theories of mystery presence. Eliade applies his studies of the history of religions to Judeo-Christianity, as in the sentence: "Judeo-Christianity was the transfiguration of History into theophany."[6] Eliade defines myth as the narration of a primordial event that took place at the beginning, and he likes to link this to the phrase once used in the Roman liturgy to introduce the day's gospel reading: *in illo tempore* ("at that time").[7] This phrase appeals to him because he sees ritual as the continuous repetition of the original Christ-event, in a way comparable to the way ancient rite reenacted the original mythical story of the beginnings. The difference is that ancient myths and rites dealt with cyclic time, with an eternal return, whereas Judeo-Christianity is historical and turns history itself into a theophany. Therefore, the repetition of the Christian mystery in ritual does not bring us back to a cycle of time but into a time rooted in its beginning that is going forward to the eschaton. Still Eliade's view of Christian ritual is very similar to his view of ancient ritual, since for him it allows participants to remain in the sacred realm which is manifested in history in Jesus Christ.

Comparing Christian liturgy to an imitation and reenactment of mysteries was used in patristic times to teach the faithful, especially in what is known to us as mystagogical catechesis, though there does seem to have been a split between this and their more refined theology.[8] In catechesis, the various points of ritual were explained to neophytes as images and imitations of Christ's death, descent into hell, and resurrection. While the Bible received most attention in precatechumenal catechesis, the rites were explained in mystagogical catechesis, with abundant use of Old Testament figures and natural symbolism to relate them to Christ's mysteries.

With his notion of the metamorphosis of natural sacredness through the incarnation, Louis Bouyer takes up this paradigm of religious myth and rite's relation to it, but modifies considerably what was said in the Maria Laach school.[9] Following the pattern of religious myth and its representation of a sacred and higher reality that is a model for human beings, Bouyer presents Jesus Christ as eternal man because he is the Word of God. The humanity of Jesus within the eternal Word is manifested in history through the incarnation as the presence of God among us. Bouyer explains the occurrence of mythic features in the gospels as the use of the language of natural sacredness to proclaim this supernatural mystery.[10]

According to Bouyer rites and hierophanies, that is, manifestations of sacred power in phenomena and things of nature, precede myth as a recognition of a sacred view of the universe. Myth completes this inchoate sense of the holy by offering a story and a comprehensive view of reality. Rite then becomes the representation and reenactment of what is presented in the myth. Rites on their own easily degenerate into a kind of magic. By proclaiming a higher reality to which to relate it, myth reclaims rite to its original purpose.

The difference between biblical religion and other ancient religions is the replacement of the cyclic by the historical. For this reason, Bouyer does not make a simple transition from the idea of Christ as metamorphosis of the sacred, and from the comparison

116

of the revealed Word with myth, to the idea of liturgy as reenactment and imitation of Christ's mysteries. In this, he separates himself from Odo Casel, for he sees nothing in Christian liturgy which can be called an imitation of Christ's mysteries in the manner in which mystery religions had rites that imitated the story of the gods. His explanation of the relation of ritual to the gospel word is more circumspect. He explains that because in Christ the eternal Word is made manifest, and in his flesh there is a perfect union between the divine and the human, the word that accompanies ritual is invested with a power to make present in the eucharist the self-oblation of Christ, and in the other sacraments the sanctifying power of Christ and the grace of his passion. Through the power of Christ's words in the *berakah*, the church's sacrifice of praise, his sacrifice is made present, not in imitation but in the reality of his self-offering and in the reality of the transformation of humanity and creation that comes about in the incarnation. The result is that to rites to which humanity naturally attributes a sacred meaning, such as a meal or water immersion, the word of God brings in the name of Christ a transforming power.[11]

This explanation removes any notion that liturgical rites are the imitation or figural representation of Christ's death and resurrection. It inserts the rites into the prayer of thanksgiving, the *berakah*, which is the church's proper response to the proclaimed word. The incarnation is viewed, however, as an eternal reality manifested in the flesh and proclaimed in the gospel. No clear explanation is given of how the narrative that leads to thanksgiving fits into the memorial action, other than by way of motivation.

The model of the Aristotelian *mythos* and *mimesis* as taken up by literary critics gives some insight into this, and also gives a different perspective on how God is revealed in Jesus Christ and a different perspective on

117

history, or the time between the historical Christ and the second coming.[12] This model has six advantages for liturgy: (1) it allows more attention to be given to the human quality of Jesus' actions, with less emphasis on their nature as actions of the Logos; (2) it allows a reading of narrative "from the end"; (3) it allows a vision of history as an anticipation rather than as an acting out of a divine plan; (4) it associates memorial with memory rather than with ritual imitation; (5) it makes it possible to include events after Christ into liturgical narrative, according to a model of generative poetics and use of historical master images; and (6) it allows a clearer perception of Christian ritual's relation to narrative.

In this model, myth and traditional narrative are used almost interchangeably. This form is looked upon as a type of literature concerning human actions, not with a story of the gods.[13] It represents human action as typical, representative of a common or ideal way of being as realized in the story told. This narrative form is not used to describe an act or set of actions in factual detail; it is an ideal narrative, a somewhat abstract though concrete presentation of what is fundamental and archetypal in human action. Thus it proffers a meaning for human life where this ideal type of behavior is imitated or taken as normative. It operates "at the top level of human desire,"[14] expressing what human beings are encouraged to seek as meaningful and desirable, even if not always attainable, and what they consider to be right conduct in the kind of situation described in the story. The myth is often fictional, in the sense that it deals with imaginary characters, but it is true in the sense that it represents ideal values and meaning, something to be sought and followed. It is not the story of the gods which is the prototype of myth understood in this way, but such classical stories as the Oedipus myth. With what it includes of the abstract and the ideal, the form can be

118

used to narrate history or the story of particular persons, when these are presented for what they reveal about the universal and the ideal, or when they give the plot of an ideal human reality.

Typically, this kind of narrative is to be interpreted from the end rather than from the beginning, for the resolution of the plot dictates its development from the beginning. It is not the story of a divine redeemer or some heroic figure coming from another realm to bring something into the world, but the story of human persons who deal in darkness with the conflict and struggle of life, yet who still come to an ideal resolution as envisaged in the narrative, so that all their actions can reveal truth and meaning in virtue of their openness to this end. Thus one can distinguish between the tragic plot with its tragic but heroic ending, the comic plot with its happy ending, the romantic plot with its quest finally fulfilled, and the ironic plot whose ending parodies the romantic, for what was sought and is gained turns out to be a thing of straw.[15]

The sense of anticipation in the story, or in the deeds narrated, is keen, not because the central figure knows the end but because that character consciously pursues action to an end. This end is somehow implied in the performance of right action, or even in the mistakes made because of ignorance of some vital factors, as when Oedipus sleeps with his mother and kills his father. Classical myths often present this unyielding movement toward an end as Fate, especially in tragic plots, where consent to Fate is a primary virtue in the tragic hero. Comic plot allows the central figure to foresee a good ending, even if ignorant of what that ending is, for this hero is confident that even immediate or apparent catastrophe will be set in perspective by the ultimate fulfillment of desire.

Some critics affirm that this kind of plot and narrative is verified in the way the gospels tell the story of Jesus

Christ, but that these same gospels had an important influence on subsequent Western literature because of the ways in which they depart from classical stories.[16] A similar pattern of ideal action and resolution of conflicts is found in the ending, but the story of Jesus as told in the gospels is much more realistic than classical myths. His story has a clear place in the daily life of people, and mundane and simple human actions are incorporated into it. Jesus himself is not some grand hero but belongs quite naturally among peasants and the lower classes. The story is closer to comedy than tragedy because it is the *divina commedia,* but it includes elements of the tragic. Its genius is to present model and representative plot together with a boldness of lively detail which reflects the lives of simple and ordinary people.

When the narrative is interpreted along these lines, Jesus is remembered for his experience of God as "Abba" and for his fidelity in continuing to proclaim the advent of God's kingdom among the poor even to the point of giving witness in death.[17] As an ending to the story, the resurrection gives evidence of God's fidelity to Jesus even in death, and of the confirmation of the kingdom which he preached. The story leads to the climax of a double fidelity, that of Jesus to God and of God to Jesus. This narrative is remembered in the church as an ideal story, one in which the typical presentation of Jesus as Redeemer, Master, and Lord takes precedence over factual detail, but which still incorporates a considerable amount of such detail. To follow Jesus, or to imitate Christ, is to share his experience of God as "Abba," to be assured of his own presence in the church as Lord, and to confront life's necessities and tragedies in the same trust in God's promise, in anticipation of that end to history which is promised and foreshadowed in the resurrection. The church lives in anticipation of the kingdom, and this constitutes its way of being in the world. Faithfulness to Jesus' teaching is integrated into a participation in history as anticipation, rather than into an acceptance of a teaching in which the fullness of truth is already given. The teleological character of the Jesus story is brought out in this appreciation of its narrative form, and consequently brought out is the teleological quality of a remembrance by the church of his life, death, and resurrection.

From this angle, it is possible to envisage the relation between memorial and memory. The difficulty with the model of the incarnation as transformation of sacred myth is that it presents the story of Christ as essentially complete, one which when accepted leads to the eternal life which it forecasts. Memory appears as a look backward for an ideal to follow, and ritual memorial represents past events whose completeness is celebrated. The Aristotelian model of narrative includes more shadow and calls for the anticipatory character of memory, a remembering of the past in virtue of what is anticipated in the future as fulfillment of desire.[18]

Insight into human consciousness, its structure and its drive, can affect understanding of liturgical memorial. The holy is more likely to be revealed in human action, with its innate drive to self-transcendence, than in theophany. Memory and keeping memory are an interiorization of narrative. Augustine made an unsurpassed contribution to a Christian understanding of memory when he connected faith in the mystery of Christ with knowledge of the self.[19] To contemplate the eternal verities revealed in Christ, one must go back in memory to one's own beginnings. As a Manichean Augustine had sought his preexistence in the world of darkness, and as a neo-Platonist he was tempted to see it in a world of ideas. As a Christian, believing in creation out of nothing, he became aware of the contingency of his existence, of the nothing out of

which the human creature comes. To confront this
nothingness, he placed himself before the Word of
God, without whom nothing was made and in whose
image he then knew himself to be fashioned. To go
back to one's beginnings in memory, to discover there
the yearning for eternity, for the true and the good, is
to go back to the Word. Since this same Word spoke in
history from the very creation of the world and in the
fullness of time in Jesus Christ, the recollection of the
Word, in whose image the self is made, is also the
memory of world history in which the Word spoke, or
was uttered. The memorialization of the Pasch in
worship and the memory of one's own beginnings,
with insight into the nature of the mind, coincide. The
contemplation of the Word in history is also the
contemplation of the Word in whose image the human
person is made.

This understanding of memory is a major step on the
way of interiorization, but still it does not give enough
place to hope as an anticipation of desire's fulfillment,
or to the teleology of the human spirit. Memory is
much more a look back in virtue of what one
anticipates in desire, than in virtue of what one sees by
foreknowledge. The interiorization which guides
memory of Jesus Christ comes in touch with aspirations
and their projection of a future. One can see how this
links up with the nature of the narrative as an
anticipation of the kingdom, a promise symbolized in
the resurrection. The Christ story is remembered as an
event which took place in time and which revealed the
anticipation of God's kingdom as the meaning of
history. It is a narrative which becomes memorial when
conjoined with the act of memory whereby a
community finds in it the anticipation of its own
yearnings, which take shape through trust in the God
of promise revealed in Jesus. In other words, memorial
is a dialectic between the recall of the narrative and the
purification of the desire inherent to a memory which

has its roots in interiority and which by the gift of the Spirit prompts one to self-transcendence.

Since the story of Christ is presented as public and typical, it is a story which unites communities of all ages and places. Since the story lays claim to factual truth, it is remembered as one guaranteed by divine testimony and so as a clear act of revelation. It is a revelation of humanity's being, whereby we are called to live in trust in God, and of God's being, which is faithful Love. Neither being is known in fullness. For this, we await in anticipation for the coming of the kingdom.

Augustine took the preexistent Word, who descended and ascended, as the image of both self and history. This relates history to a vertical, supraterrestrial model, something eternal and omnitemporal which precedes the history in which it is manifested. Though he endeavored to tie this in with an intrahistorical chain of events, it was difficult to look for insight into the events themselves, since they were always to be judged in the light of the divine prototype. Looking to the anticipation of the kingdom in the Christ-event gives a different measure to memory and has a clearer relation to the present, in those experiences lived by a believing community. This would mean two tasks for liturgical narrative, two tasks which could be included under the term "generative poetics." A first task would be to narrate the story of Christ in new ways more culturally related to the community, even while always looking back to the gospels as starting point and criterion. This would mean selecting images and metaphors taken from cultural riches. In their hymnic style and use of imagery, some of the New Testament hymns, for example Philippians 2 and Colossians 1, could be seen as examples of a Christian community using imagery from its cultural background to recall the essential events of Christ's death and exaltation. It is unlikely that these hymns belonged to common worship, but nonetheless they are good examples of an adoption of cultural images in remembering, as befits the hymnic mode. The same could be said of the narrative section of some of the early eucharistic prayers, especially Eastern and Syrian, as far as the memorial element in blessing is concerned. We are also led to believe that some Christian liturgies kept a moment of recounting and remembering Christ which has affinities with the Jewish *Haggadah*.[20]

A second task of generative poetics would be to include events and persons after Christ within the Christian story, presenting them as imitations of Christ and in similar ways anticipations of the kingdom. There are some passing attempts to do this in the inclusion of the Acts of the Martyrs in the liturgy,[21] in the prefaces of the Verona Sacramentary with their attention to current happenings, and in the new Roman Sacramentary's prefaces for saints. The Verona prefaces turn all too readily to petition, however, and the modern ones are stereotyped and flat.

HISTORICAL MASTER IMAGES[22]
One way in which generative poetics functions is through a creative use of historical master images, which have an archetypal function within a tradition. Such images come from the historical experience of a people and its interpretation. They are born out of an event, the meaning of which they interpret and signify, including its power for the future. Master images are woven into the account of further historical events and can serve to interpret the significance of current experiences. They develop as they are used.

An example from profane history is the notion of human rights, which has taken on symbolic properties. It originated with the Virginia bill of rights in 1776 and entered a wider history via the American Declaration of

Independence and the French Revolution. While the term referred originally to a specific set of rights pertaining to a particular situation, in time it has taken on a more vast import. As a notion it has exercised considerable influence in the shaping of modern history. This influence is due partly to the historical circumstances in which the notion arose and partly to its frequent renewal in new situations, such as the founding of the United Nations and its declaration of rights.

One example of historical master image in the Bible is that of exile. The symbol derives from the experience of leaving one's own land. As we have already seen in Chapter 4, it is one of the images accompanying that of sin. With its counterimage of return, it served to interpret the deliverance of the people of Israel from the land of Egypt. It was then used throughout Israel's history, describing the whole gamut of the people's relations with God. Other such images that occur in the scriptures are covenant, kingdom, Jerusalem as God's dwelling place, and the *ekklesia* of God's people.

The effectiveness and meaning of these symbols change with historical experience, but they always keep their roots in previous history and evoke it whenever used.[23] Sometimes the change in meaning is quite deliberate, using past evocations to refer to new situations in a startling way. This is the case with Jesus' use of the symbol of kingdom, or in the use that the gospel writers make of it in reference to him. Because of its historical usage, the image referred to the hope of a people, either to the hope of the restoration of the kingdom of Israel or to the apocalyptic expectations which had replaced this hope. In the preaching of Jesus and in the gospels it refers to a personal history, that of Jesus and his followers. Its social aspect no longer has anything to do with an earthly kingdom, but instead refers to the experience of a fellowship of disciples who accept the values expressed in the preaching of Jesus about God's reign. Later in the hands of the church, the symbol became identified with the church and even with the hierarchical church. Since the symbol always keeps its roots in the tradition, it is always open to reinterpretation, which can break its current use so that it can be opened to the transforming power of its historical potential. In recent decades, this seems to have happened to the symbol of kingdom as used in the Roman Catholic Church. Its reference to the hierarchical church has been broken. In a closer reading of the gospel, it may now refer to the experience of discipleship and to the hope of liberation from enslavement and victimization which is carried by such texts as the Beatitudes.

Using historical master images, then, requires imaginative discourse, one that through a fresh and inspired use of the image and story shocks the hearer into realizing life's potencies.[24] Human nature tends to inhabit a world of unproductive images that have a purely representative or figurative function, that illustrate things all too familiar, or that keep people in the immediate world of sense perception. They are pure reminders, like the family photographs on the dining-room wall. They have no creative force other than a passing evocation of sentiment and nostalgia. This has been the way verbal and visual images have been used, and sacramental symbols themselves have been reduced to that role. In the celebration of the eucharist, the narrative of the death of Jesus no longer shocks. It no longer gives rise to prayers of thanksgiving that are imaginative expressions of what it is to receive the power of that death in the present, where the struggle is against injustice and forgetfulness. Instead, what is uppermost in the tenor of many a celebration is the dogma of transubstantiation, supported by the static images that encourage naive realism.

126

When imagination is active, and this is the only proper response to the power of traditional images, it no longer functions as pure reminder but serves as interpreter. In interpreting, it projects a new range of experiences and hopes. To reach this point, it is necessary to break the accepted representative range of the image. The picture on the wall is not just grandfather at the age of 70, disconsolately awaiting death. It is a man of the soil who has fought all the struggles of providing for a family and fighting the extortions of landlords in a time of famine. Similarly, the oil of anointing is more than a sign of grace in sickness. It is surrounded by texts that evoke all the history of kings, priests, prophets, and martyrs, all the cries and tears and the full-throated exultation of the Anointed of God.

This creative use of historical images in storytelling and prayer is essential to project a future that is inseparable from memory and memorial. One can make five-year plans for economic recovery, but only in the language of the imagination, in a creative look back to origins, can deep hopes and prospects be expected. The energy to seek freedom, to hope for liberation, to commit oneself to solidarity with the oppressed and victimized of human systems, this type of energy and trust comes only through the language of imaginative projection. It allows the church to speak beyond its knowing of the future. It is an essential part of remembering and retelling the story of Jesus Christ in hope.

NARRATIVE AND RITE

As already remarked, the ritual used in Christian liturgy is not of a nature to be associated with cosmic and life-cycle rites, nor does it fit neatly with the hierophany of sacred places and things. Rather, it is of a nature to symbolize the mode of a daily fellowship in faith, where ordinary activities and simple services reveal the Lord's presence among the people. Nothing in the most central acts of Christian liturgy or sacrament would allow us to call them an imitation or representation in figurative form of Christ's death, descent into the tomb, and resurrection. Allegorical interpretation reads this kind of meaning into the ceremonies of the liturgy, but that is not their symbolic meaning, that is, the second meaning given in the first. The taking, breaking, and sharing of bread represent a mode of fellowship, and because it is such a fellowship, the presence of the Lord is recognized and proclaimed. The one action of the Lord which is repeated and represented is that of his sharing bread and cup with his disciples, as a way of sharing in the salvation which comes through his death. The action of the Supper thus unites a memorial narrative with a rite which symbolizes directly a community, a way of being in the unity of faith and charity, a unity which is such because the members are nourished by the Lord's body and blood. The people recall the death in the narrative and the gift of the body and blood in the distribution of the bread and the passing of the cup. This means that within the symbolism of the meal a second symbolism occurs, which is of the type known as metonymy. In the bread and wine, the Lord gives his own body and blood. The Lord's presence and the gift of the Spirit are assured because the people receive the gift of the body and blood.

Two remarks can be made about this symbolism whereby the people participate in the death through the reception of the body and blood in the bread and wine. First, we can relate the two meanings of the meal ritual, the one which refers to the community, the other which refers to the Lord's body and blood given as gift. The relation reveals the nonidentity which is proper to symbolism. The Lord who is one with the community, so that it can even be called his body or his sacrament, is nonetheless not identical with it. His presence as gift and promise in the bread and wine is as much a symbol of absence as it is of presence. In other words, the gift of the body and blood is the symbolism of presence in a community with which he is nonetheless not to be totally identified, even when quite rightly the images of body and sacrifice may be so inclusive as to refer simultaneously and corporately to the Lord and to the people, who have become one in the power of the Spirit.

Second, it is not an imitation of the death which is retained in the symbolism of bread and wine, although it gives a share in that death. It is true that some exegesis of the New Testament suggests that the breaking of the bread was a prophetic action of Jesus foretelling his death, and the pouring out of the cup a prophetic action representing the shedding of his blood.[25] This prophetic action, if separated from the accompanying words, could easily give a basis for the allegorical turn that is found in later sacramental catechesis or theology. One must remember, however, that it depends on the more fundamental symbolism of the fellowship in faith and mutual service. If Jesus did attach some prophetic significance to the gesture, it would depend on the narratives of God's salvation which he and his disciples would have been accustomed to hearing and repeating.

Similar remarks need to be made about the other sacraments, especially about baptism, where the proclivity to see the baptismal act as figurative of the Lord's mysteries is greatest. What is directly signified or symbolized is the life of the community, or the purification and new life which persons receive when professing faith in Jesus as Lord as they are taken into the life of the community. The metonymy that occurs within this symbolism is that of grace or the Spirit present in the water. This signifies both the grace or the Spirit received and the nonidentity of this grace or

Spirit with the community in which it is received. The Lord's power is always pure gift; it always transcends the church in which it is actualized. Any imitation of the Lord's death, descent into hell, or resurrection is secondary to this symbolism. The well-known text of Romans 6 does not seem to refer to an action to be read as an imitation of Jesus' death, but speaks rather of the total communion with Jesus in his death which comes about in baptism, a communion which results in a share in the life of the resurrection.

In brief, it can be said that memorial in Christian liturgy is constituted by both narrative and ritual and by their interaction. The narrative serves as the means for an active remembering of Christ's mysteries and an active projection of the hope of the kingdom. The rite encompasses the community and signifies the mode of being of a people who keep this memory as a source of life and hope. Something of the meaning of the narrative transfers to the rite, not by way of an imitation of what is narrated but by way of metonymy, whereby the presence of the Lord and the power of the Spirit in the community are signified. This signification is such as to underscore the nature of the Lord's presence as free gift and the nonidentity of Lord and Spirit with the community which they enliven and through which they are present to the world.

METAPHOR[26]

We have seen how cosmic hierophany and ritual are absorbed into liturgy by the conjunction of verbal symbols that appeal to this experience with simple rites of homely worship and care. We have also seen how the form of religious myth gives way to myths which are human stories, whether the universal history of the Adamic myth or the particular history of universal import of Jesus Christ. In those stories, remembering and anticipation complete one another. We have also seen how the narrative is received within a community

130

that uses the rites of domestic worship, so that the economy and ordinariness of the rite is complemented by the economy and ordinariness of the narrative. All of this involves moving from hierophany to word in the manifestation of the holy, and a concomitant move from cosmic to homely ritual, from a myth of the gods to the myth or narrative of human action in which God is present and active. It is now possible to suggest that the key to this economic revelation of the holy is metaphor, or more fully, the metaphorical process.

The word "metaphor" may cause some to think of comparisons that are so trite and commonplace as to carry little weight, as when it is said that an angry man bellows like a lion. Even traditional Christian metaphors, such as shepherd or king, seem to illustrate ideas or dogmas rather than convey new and fresh insights into reality. If this were all that metaphor did, it would serve no great purpose to introduce it into this context.

Unfortunately, we are accustomed to hearing dead metaphors, which at best serve as rhetoric in the art of persuasion, and even more often are dropped casually into passing conversation. Only if we hearken to live metaphors, catch them at the moment of their introduction, can we appreciate their significance. Perhaps some thought about a traditional biblical metaphor would be rewarding before making more technical observations about the nature of metaphor. "Blessed are you poor, for yours is the kingdom of God" is a metaphor, because it names something by a very unlikely name. The blessedness that God promises to the poor, to the outcasts, to the little people of Jewish society at Jesus' time is described by the name that the people used when they hoped for the restoration of the glory of Davidic times. Leaders, the powerful, warriors, great teachers, were the ones with whom to associate the restoration of the kingdom, not women, children, peasants, fisherfolk, the leprous, and the unwashed. Putting the poor and the kingdom together is a conjunction of opposites, a startling revelation which Christians have yet to fathom after many centuries.

In explaining metaphor, one must first break beyond what is called the substitution theory, which concentrates on the resemblance between two things, but ignores the force of predication in context that occurs when metaphors are spoken. Only dead metaphors, where the resemblance is taken for granted, can be carried at will into a context. Living metaphor gives its meaning in the context within which it is uttered. The truth of the substitution theory is that metaphors concern resemblance and call something by a name that is not proper to it but to something else. In that sense, one would say that "the lion is the king of animals" and "the Lord is my shepherd" are metaphorical statements, for neither king nor shepherd properly belongs to its subject in these predications. A likeness is presumed to justify the predication. In making metaphors, an eye for resemblances is required, just as in hearing them one is supposed to look for the resemblance.

Neglected in the substitution theory is the meaning that comes from the context, and the resemblance that is predicated of what at first seem to be very unlike. Metaphor is then the assertion of new meaning, not the predication of a likeness and meaning already evident. The comparison comes then as a shock, although one which in its surprise carries recognition of the truth of the comparison. Not all writers on metaphor see the degree of shock or startling revelation in the same way, and of course it is an open question whether literary metaphors and biblical metaphors can be considered in the same fashion. That depends on the degree to which God's word and intervention are seen to be in keeping with, or at variance with, what would be naturally expected.[27] It is not necessary, however, to resolve such disputes to see how metaphors open up and change our vision of reality.

Philip Wheelwright offers the example of this line of poetry:

I walked abroad
And saw the round moon lean over a hedge,
Like a red-faced farmer.
I did not stop to talk, but nodded;
And round about were the wistful stars
With white faces like town children.
(T. E. Hulme, "Autumn"[28])

When one is used to mystic odes to the moon and normally surrounds it with mystery and majesty, the comparison to a red-faced farmer leaning over the hedge is startling. Yet it resonates such that we recognize our familiarity with the moon and with the familiar way in which the moon introduces an aura of country freshness into our city lives and industrial complexes. T. S. Eliot's use of the image of the Waste Land to describe our self-satisfied and progressive twentieth century is also a shock, but one that rings true.[29]

In a metaphor, then, there is a yoking of unlikes, a comparison which can be made only on the assumption of difference, so that the resemblance appears within the difference. An interaction and a tension between key terms result, with a resultant new meaning. The new meaning has a twist to it, putting in conjunction recognizable opposites. Only in the context is the apparent conflict of meanings resolved and something comes to be known which would not otherwise appear.

The point is often made[30] that metaphor unveils the meaning of the ordinary rather than of the extraordinary, or at least makes the extraordinary appear within the ordinary. It is in the limited, the finite, the mundane, that good metaphor unfolds new meaning and shows up new possibilities of being. It delves *into* the mundane and the accustomed circumstances of life to show what lies hidden there. Metaphor redescribes reality in order to create it anew[31] by the power of revealing speech. What is more, even though it concerns particulars, metaphor carries a note of universality. In the line of poetry where Eliot conjures up the image of measuring out time with coffee spoons,[32] the dry futility of such existence fits many another way of life besides one spent waiting vainly for visitors at a tea table.

The metaphor as a figure of speech occurs within a sentence, a sentence having a context. Strictly speaking, this predication is what grammarians know as metaphor. From what is perceived to occur when such predication is made, however, one can talk of the metaphorical in a story or a ritual, when the tensive bringing together of unlikes results not from a single sentence but from the larger context of the story or ritual as a unit. Metaphor in this larger sense makes new and odd connections which afford insight into reality and thus transform our experience of it.

From James Joyce's *A Portrait of the Artist as a Young Man*, one can take examples of three types of the metaphorical. First, there is a single sentence: "I go . . . to forge in the smithy of my soul the uncreated conscience of my race."[33] Here the metaphor is the resemblance posited between a smithy, who forges implements of farming or industry, and the craft of the young, inexperienced writer. The future is supposed to be built on technical skill and hard work, of which the smithy is the image, so that the metaphor makes large claims for the influence of the writer who probes the depths of his own and his nation's consciousness and influences the world through the use of words.

The second example of the metaphorical is a situation described at some length,[34] a prosaic situation in which the text unveils hidden presences and realities. Stephen Daedulus, the protagonist, and his fellow students are at a rather dull lecture on physics given by a Jesuit professor. Prompted by the rude humor of one of the other students, Stephen's fantasy conjures up a motley of Jesuits engaged in various enterprises, possessed of different turns of character, doing a medley of tasks, combining the dignified and the clownish, all tumbling together like priestly vestments hanging on a wall and blown about by a gust of wind "in a sabbath of misrule." Somehow, this astute and colorful camaraderie of the Jesuits is present even in the dull lecture of the physics professor. In this case the metaphorical links Stephen's vision of the order with the lecture that is so commonplace.

The third example of the metaphorical is the book itself as a unit, the things that are linked together by the plot. Out of the humdrum, the poverty of the family, the ineffectualness of the parents, the endangered schooling, the dowdiness and garrulousness of life in Dublin and in the provinces, the rude companionship and dull teachers, the tawdry religion and quarrelsome nationalism, an artist comes forth with a vision of life and a use of words that are destined to have universal impact.

From this example, one may conjecture the various ways in which the metaphor is key to liturgical symbolism, in its manifestation of the divine in the human, the transcendence in the act, the awesomeness of the ordinary, the specificity of the Christian. Six points will be made about this.

First, when biblical scholars address themselves to the issue of metaphor, they are wont to take the gospel parables as the primary example.[35] Within a story rather than in a single sentence, and in a story about very ordinary situations of human life in the time of Jesus, contrasts and conjunctions are made that reveal the presence of the kingdom of God in the world and its effect on human life. A much-quoted case is that of the father and his two sons, the prodigal and the stay-at-home (Luke 15). For the hearers the situation was easily recognizable, but the father's conduct toward the two young men is unexpected and unusual. This unexpectedness carries a message about forgiveness and about justice or uprightness of life as these belong within the kingdom that Jesus preached. Since the liturgy celebrates the presence of God in daily life and the transformation of ordinary experience, the parabolic has a permanent place therein. The horizons of faith and immersion in daily activity mesh within the liturgy.

The second point is that the entire story of Jesus which is commemorated is metaphorical, in that it presents *him* as the one in whom the promises of the kingdom are fulfilled. This is an extraordinary transfer of religious, national, and apocalyptic hopes, of powerful names and images, to one whose life is lived among the simple and the poor, whose teaching proclaims the values encouched in the Beatitudes, who serves rather than being served, and whose only power is the love and trust shown in the meekness of his death. The kingdom is revealed in the concreteness of his deeds and of his teaching. It is a story that would not be the same if it did not include the parables and the sayings. All this is done within the horizon of the kingdom, of the universal, of the conflict between God's power and satanic powers.[36]

Third, the ritual or bodily element in liturgy is metaphorical. As we have seen, Christian liturgy is removed from the cosmic and is remarkably simple, even domestic. A contrast exists between the simplicity of the rites and the cosmic images that carry over into it. The paradox or metaphor of this ritual is that it is taken to represent the holiness and power of God among the people and in the world, whereas hierophany and cosmic ritual are the more instinctive ways to perceive these. In Christian worship, those things and actions which are directly representative of the ordinary and the daily are proclaimed by word to be the symbols of God's presence and action.

Fourth, there is metaphorical usage in the way the cultic terms are predicated of the Christian people, and then in a second moment only of their worship, even though the usage contrasts with the context and ritual from which the terms are originally taken. In the New Testament, cultic terms such as priesthood, sacrifice, and temple are never used of acts of worship, such as the Lord's Supper and baptism. Instead, they are used to designate the people who are made holy in Christ, to designate the preaching of the gospel, to describe a life of obedience to the gospel, or to apply to Christ giving his life for our redemption.[37] This is a transfer of language from one order of things, that of solemn and priestly ritual, to another, that of life in the Spirit and of deeds done in obedience to God. In early patristic times, there is some transfer of these terms back to Christian worship, but only by way of contrast. Thus the great prayer of thanksgiving in the eucharist is called a sacrifice, as is the act of baptism, or the entire eucharistic action. Terms which rightly belong in an order of things where blood rituals, the offering of material things, and ritual purifications prevail are being used to designate a prayer or actions which signify the community's remembrance of Jesus Christ and its life in the Spirit.

Fifth, there is probably much work to be done to bring to the surface the metaphors of liturgical euchology and action, where the meaning depends on the context and the contrasts made. Some examples may be quoted. In the prayer of anointing of the sick, anointing signifies in the first place the care of the community and the Lord's healing power active in it. Yet, in due time the euchology of the sacrament applies the image of one anointed to the sick person who supports the illness in faith and who is added to the throng of kings, prophets, priests, and martyrs. This is to move from a significance which concerns healing to a significance which concerns supporting illness in faith, but the two continue to exist side by side, neither being eliminated. In marriage, the mystical imagery of love between Christ and the church is predicated of simple acts of human tenderness and fleshly union. In ordination, social power and authority are transformed through the use of images of service.

Sixth, the confession of sins is central to the appropriation of metaphorical language. It is the moment when individuals or communities see their lives transformed by grace and by bringing to language the grace which they find operative in their lives. This brings together the language of grace and the language necessary to describe daily events of one's life and action. A double contrast exists in confession: that between grace and the ordinary, and that between grace and sin. The revised order of penance for the Roman Rite describes confession, based on contrition, as seeing one's life from the perspective of God's mercy and love.[38] Not every confession of sins reaches the heights of Augustine's, but in many respects the *Confessions* will ever remain the paradigm for confession. Augustine was able to bring together a scrutiny of his life with the understanding of grace which he found in the mystery of the incarnation. To know himself, he had to know God as he was made known in the Word made flesh. To know God, he had to know himself. The *Confessions* express a vision of God's grace in his own life, in some of the most minute and trivial of his actions, in the transformation of his outlook, and even in the mercy with which he himself could look on the deeds and events of his past. The experience of life becomes totally different when it is transformed into a life lived in the knowledge of God's mercy, breaking the boundaries of limit and sin, making daily events and immersion in human enterprise actions in which God's grace and the hope of God's kingdom are embodied. Confession expresses what is perhaps the greatest contrast of all in Christian life: though we must probe our consciences, come to know ourselves and the source of our actions, overcome our faults, and come to good action by taking consciousness, in the end we stop short in face of the enigma of our own limitations and sin, totally dependent on the healing and forgiveness that can come from God alone. This is to stop short in the face of what is the leitmotiv of Christian liturgy: where sin abounded, grace did more abound.

CONCLUSION

Discussed in this chapter was the meaning that verbal images attain or take on within the context of story. First, we described generally what is meant by myth and how it determines the meaning of the images it assumes. Then we spoke of the Adamic myth and of how it provides a continuing base to liturgical celebration. It brings to language the universal experience of sin and the universal dilemma of the difference between evil for which persons are responsible and the evil which is already in the world. Third, we spoke of how the narrative of Christ's death and resurrection, or more generally of Christ's mystery, can be understood in the light of an Aristotelian understanding of *mythos* which has been taken over by literary criticism. This served to explain how this mystery is represented in the liturgy. Finally, we took metaphor as the key to understanding how images are assumed into narrative and ritual so that new meaning is expressed and reality created anew.

1. Philip Wheelwright, in *Metaphor and Reality* (Bloomington: Indiana University Press, 1962), p. 239, gives this definition: "Myth is to be defined as a complex of stories—some no doubt fact, and some fantasy—which, for various reasons, human beings regard as demonstrations of the inner meaning of the universe and of human life." On the origins of myth and its relation to other modes of discourse, see Susanne K. Langer, *Philosophy in a New Key: A Study in the Symbolism of Reason, Rite, and Art*, 3rd ed. (Cambridge, Mass.: Harvard University Press, 1978), pp. 171–203.

2. Paul Ricoeur, *The Symbolism of Evil* (Boston: Beacon Press, 1967).

3. Beatriz Melano Couch, "Religious symbols and philosophical reflection," in Charles E. Reagan (ed.), *Studies in the Philosophy of Paul Ricoeur* (Athens: Ohio University Press, 1979), p. 121: "Ricoeur points out a threefold function of the myth . . . 1. Represent by means of symbolic language concrete universal human experience; 2. Introduce a historical tension in this experience (there is a beginning and an end); 3. Explore the cleavage between innocence and guilt."

4. *Le Pontifical Romano-Germanique du Dixième Siécle*, ed. C. Vogel & R. Elze, 2 vols. (Vatican City: Vatican Press, 1963).

5. Odo Casel, *The Mystery of Christian Worship* (Westminster, Md.: Newman Press, 1962).

6. Mircea Eliade, *Images and Symbols* (London: Harvill, 1961), p. 164.

7. Mircea Eliade, *The Sacred and the Profane: The Nature of Religion* (New York & London: Harcourt Brace & World, 1959), p. 95: "The myth relates a sacred history, that is, a primordial event that took place at the beginning of time, *ab initio.* . . . The myth is the history of what took place *in illo tempore*, the recital of what the gods or the semidivine beings did at the beginning of time. . . ."

8. Hugh M. Riley, *Christian Initiation* (Washington, D.C.: Catholic University of America Press, 1974).

9. Louis Bouyer, *Rite and Man: Natural Sacredness and Christian Liturgy* (Notre Dame, Ind.: University of Notre Dame

Press, 1963), p. 11: "The Incarnation does not lead to the disappearance of natural sacredness but to its metamorphosis."

10. Ibid., p. 219: "If the Christian message, like every other religious message, finds its natural and necessary expression in concepts that are of mythic origins . . . it does not do so without making a radical split in the natural structure of myth itself. . . . It did this by substituting for the cyclic vision of the universe, in which the same powers ceaselessly reproduce the same invariable order of phenomena, a really transcendent intervention which, by means of a unique saving event, effected a definitive modification in reality."

11. Ibid., pp. 95–122. These ideas are developed further in *Le Père Invisible.*

12. Stephen Crites, "The narrative quality of experience," *Journal of the American Academy of Religion* 39 (1971), 291–311; Northrop Frye, *Anatomy of Criticism* (Princeton, N.J.: Princeton University Press, 1957), and "New directions from old," in Henry A. Murray (ed.), *Myth and Mythmaking* (Boston: Beacon Press, 1960), pp. 115–31; Robert Scholes & Robert Kellogg, *The Nature of Narrative* (New York: Oxford University Press, 1966).

13. Frye, "New directions from old," p. 117: "The verbal imitation of ritual is myth, and the typical action of poetry is the plot, or what Aristotle calls *mythos,* so that for the literary critic the Aristotelian term *mythos* and the English word myth are much the same thing. Such plots, because they describe typical actions, naturally fall into typical forms." See Frye, *Anatomy of Criticism,* pp. 82–83, 104–5.

14. Frye, *Anatomy of Criticism,* p. 136.

15. Frye, "New directions from old," p. 117.

16. Eric Auerbach, *Mimesis* (Princeton: Princeton University Press, 1953), pp. 20ff.

17. This is at the heart of Schillebeeckx's Christology, *Jesus: An Experiment in Christology,* translated by Hubert Hoskins (New York: Seabury Press, 1979), 626–74.

18. On memory and narrative, see Johann B. Metz, *Faith in*

History and Society. Toward a Practical Fundamental Theology (New York: Seabury Press), pp. 88–135, 184–218; H. Weinrich, "Narrative theology," *Concilium* 85 (New York: Herder & Herder, 1973), pp. 46–56; Paul Ricoeur, "Narrative time," *Critical Inquiry* 7 (1980), 169–90; "The narrative function," *Semeia* 13 (1978), 177–202.

19. Augustine, *Confessions* X, 6–27. See John S. Dunne, *A Search for God in Time and Memory* (Notre Dame, Ind.: University of Notre Dame Press, 1977), pp. 45–56.

20. The best-known example is Melito of Sardis, *On Pascha and Fragments*, texts and translations edited by Stuart George Hall (Oxford: Oxford University Press, 1979). See the article by Georg Kretschmar, "Christliches Pascha im 2. Jahrhundert und die Ausbildung der christlichen Theologie," *Recherches de Sciences Religieuses* 60 (1972), 287–323.

21. B. de Gaiffre, "La lecture des Actes des Martyrs dans la prière liturgique en occident," *Analecta Bollandiana* 72 (1954), 134–66.

22. Ray Hart, *Unfinished Man and the Imagination* (New York: Herder & Herder, 1968), pp. 300–05.

23. On the symbol of kingdom, see Norman Perrin, "The interpretation of a biblical symbol," *Journal of Religion* 55 (1975), 348–70.

24. Hart, pp. 180–266.

25. Jacques Dupont, "Ceci est mon corps, ceci est mon sang," *Nouvelle Revue Théologique* 80 (1958), 1025–41.

26. From the extensive literature, I would mention William F. Lynch, *Christ and Apollo: The Dimensions of the Literary Imagination* (New York: New American Library, 1963); Sally McFague, *Speaking in Parables: A Study in Metaphor and Theology* (Philadelphia: Fortress Press, 1975); Paul Ricoeur, *The Rule of Metaphor* (Toronto: Toronto University Press, 1977); "Metaphor and the main problem of hermeneutics," *New Literary History* 6 (1974/75), 95–110; Mary Schaldenbrand, "Metaphoric imagination: Kinship through conflict," in Charles Reagan (ed.), *Studies in the Philosophy of Paul Ricoeur* (Athens: Ohio University Press, 1979), pp. 57–82.

27. Hans-Georg Gadamer, "Religious and poetical speaking," in Alan M. Olson (ed.), *Myth, Symbol, and Reality* (Notre Dame, Ind.: University of Notre Dame Press, 1980), p. 97: "Although almost every work of art can be experienced as a kind of provocation, such provocations are not the same work of challenge we confront in the New Testament. To understand the absolute and radical incomprehensibility of the Christian message something other is at stake than the dimensions of our self-understanding."

28. Philip Wheelwright, *Metaphor and Reality* (Bloomington: Indiana University Press, 1968), pp. 74–75.

29. T. S. Eliot, "The Waste Land," *The Complete Poems and Plays of 1909–1950* (New York: Harcourt Brace & World, 1971), pp. 37–55.

30. McFague, *Speaking in Parables*, pp. 118–44.

31. Paul Ricoeur, "Creativity in language," *Philosophy Today* 17 (1973), 97–111.

32. T. S. Eliot, "The love song of J. Alfred Prufrock," in *The Complete Poems and Plays*, p. 5.

33. James Joyce, *A Portrait of the Artist as a Young Man* (New York: Penguin, 1964), p. 253.

34. Joyce, pp. 191–92.

35. Dominic Crossan, *In Parables* (New York: Harper & Row, 1973); Norman Perrin, *The New Testament: An Introduction* (New York: Harcourt Brace Jovanovich, 1974), pp. 3–39; Dan O. Via, *The Parables: Their Literary and Existential Dimension* (Philadelphia: Fortress Press, 1967); Amos N. Wilder, *Early Christian Rhetoric: The Language of the Gospel* (New York: Harper & Row, 1964).

36. Dominic Crossan, *The Dark Interval: Towards a Theology of Story* (Niles, Ill.: Argus, 1975), pp. 123–28.

37. Robert J. Daly, *Christian Sacrifice. The Judaeo-Christian Background before Origen* (Washington, D.C.: Catholic University of America Press, 1978).

38. *The Rites of the Catholic Church* (New York: Pueblo, 1976), p. 345.

Chapter Six

The Language and Work of Faith

Liturgy is not simply a word. It is an act, an act for which symbolic language is the necessary medium, an act of faith and celebration on the part of the church, and an act of God by which the church is transformed in grace. The question raised in this chapter is whether reflection on the symbolic structure and language of liturgy allows some insight into the manner in which it is both the act of God which sanctifies and the act of the church which gives God glory. First some preliminary remarks are in order.

PRELIMINARY REMARKS
Symbolic language of its very nature requires commitment and self-involvement if it is to be taken in any other way than as an object of curiosity or study. No matter what it proposes by way of meaning and reality, it has no effect on living unless people make it their own. Furthermore, one cannot truly discuss its meaning unless one is committed to the truth of what is represented or signified. A wager is necessary, both for self-involvement and for understanding, and this wager allows one to inhabit fully the language of symbol.[1]

Christian liturgy is traditionally professed to be the action of God's Word in Christ. This is the principal reason why Christians take part. In practice, sometimes an emphasis is placed on doing one's religious duty, and minimal participation can even be imposed under

144

pain of sin. Yet, this is not the ground for an act which Christians believe transforms life.

A profound difference is often noted between adherence to any other myth, religious or secular, and adherence to the kerygma which is recalled in Christian worship. Down through the ages, a variety of explanations of liturgy have been given which draw on the mystery of the incarnation, attending therefore especially to the person of Jesus Christ active in the liturgical event. For example, Cyril of Alexandria accented the mediatorship of Christ, in whom divinity and humanity are united. The value of the liturgy comes from the assumption of all things human by the Word, including human prayer and worship, and this identification of the Word with humanity constitutes the theological shape of the liturgy.[2] The explanation of Basil of Caeserea puts more store by contemplation. Worship is a mystery in which, through the light of the Spirit, Christians contemplate the revelation of the Father in the icon of the Son, and then through the Son in the Spirit render glory to the Father.[3] Likewise from patristic times there is the explanation of John Chrysostom, whose theology centered on the activity of Jesus Christ as high priest and victim. His explanation was responsible for a way of participating in worship which attended less to thanksgiving and more to mediation, or to the church's prayer in union with Christ for mercy and forgiveness of sin.[4] In the Latin church, a twofold approach dominated. On the one hand, God descends to humanity in the Word made flesh to offer grace and redemption. Here the divine action of Christ is given attention. On the other hand, humanity ascends to the Father in the Word made flesh to beg forgiveness and to offer praise and sacrifice. Here the human action of Christ is given attention. In recent times, this approach has been reinterpreted in the personalist terms of encounter, a renewed perspective which owes most to Edward Schillebeeckx.[5]

The aim in this chapter is distinct from such explanations. The question here is what light does the symbolic structure and language of the celebration of liturgy itself cast on its nature as action of God and of the church simultaneously. The liturgy is a memorial action in which the church relates to that historical event in which God's action in history is acclaimed and acknowledged in faith. We intend to ask what its format says about the concurrence of the divine and the human. As an answer, we will formulate a general thesis and then explicate it by referring to the movement of liturgical celebration.

THESIS
The thesis reads as follows: *The liturgy is an action wherein the testimony of God is heard and appropriated, the experience of the community is transformed, and a godly presence disclosed.*[6]

This relates to what has already been said about symbols. Two things in particular can be recalled. First, we saw that it was in the nature of symbols to articulate and transform human experience. Second, symbols were said to express the ultimacy of reality and to allow for participation in this ultimacy. In this thesis, liturgy is called a hearing and appropriating of the divine testimony given in and about Jesus Christ. This transforms experience and discloses our relation to ultimacy in a godly presence.

Presupposing (but not taking for granted) the reality of being a community of disciples, each liturgical action has immediate reference to the general or to some particular experience of this community. This may be difficult to grasp for the simple reason that we are not accustomed to relate liturgical actions to other elements of community interaction and sharing. Yet, every liturgical gathering is of its nature an expression in symbol of what Christians are otherwise pursuing in

146

mutual service and common purpose. This is true from the most important act of the Lord's Supper to a gathering of two or three for morning or evening praise. In the simplest gathering, what is transformed is the fact of being together and wanting to belong together in social interaction. As this is articulated in song and praise a godly presence in the people is disclosed. The Lord's Supper is the ritualization of a shared table, which point is missed of course whenever it fails to make clear reference to table or whenever it is the only shared table of community experience. In ritualizing the shared table, with its connotations of mutual regard and service and poverty in the Lord,[7] the Supper transforms it and reveals the Lord's presence in the bread and the wine, which presence relates to that of the Spirit in the Body.

In baptism, what is transformed is the acceptance into a community of new members by rites of purification and rebirth, and what is disclosed is the gift of the Spirit. In anointing, what is ritualized and transformed is the community's care for the sick, and what is disclosed is the presence of the Risen Lord as strength and promise. In penance, what is transformed is an acknowledgment of sin, and what is disclosed is the presence of the Lord's forgiveness. In marriage, what is transformed is the union of two persons in mutual giving, according to whatever cultural customs prevail, and what is disclosed is the bond of love which unites two persons in Christ. In ordination, what is transformed is the assumption of authority necessary for social cohesion, and what is disclosed is the presence of Christ the servant in the gifts of the Spirit.

In each case cited, the symbols used refer to the more basic human experience that is integrated into the Christian, as well as to its meaning in the church.

THE SACRAMENTAL CANON
Catholic theology has often addressed the questions of the institution of the sacraments and their essential

matter and form, and has been less preoccupied about the traditional nature of other liturgical actions, generally deemed more amenable to change. However, the issue of tradition and traditional forms can be stated differently. It is not possible to discourse adequately on what is signified and on what is transformed in liturgy without considering the entire range of celebration and the interaction of the various parts of the liturgy. These complement one another not merely by way of decorative addition, but their complementarity is important to what is signified. When early Christians used terms such as *sacramentum* or *leitourgia*, these were inclusively intended and they incorporated the entire range of liturgical celebration. As already indicated, Leo the Great used *sacramentum* in a way that included the event remembered, its gospel proclamation in the liturgy, the memorial thanksgiving, the prayer of the people, and the presence of the mystery in the daily lives of the people by way of the imitation that was made possible through the celebration.[8] This perception makes it legitimate to talk of a sacramental canon which hands down to us the normative modes of celebration in ways comparable to the fixing of the scriptural canon. No reflection on what liturgy signifies is adequate if it leaves out the range of acts and modes of discourse that belong in it, and which are known to us from earliest tradition. In his work on the origins of eucharisic celebration in the *todah* of Israel, Harvey Guthrie writes of the *kanon* which is the living context of celebration and thanksgiving to which questions of orthodoxy and orthopraxis were referred in the early church.[9] This notion of a canon of prayer includes at least implicitly set forms of celebration. Reference is made here to the importance of these forms in reflecting on liturgy's significance. Narrative, thanksgiving, supplication, lamentation, ethical exhortation, and specific types of ritual constitute this canon. In biblical studies it has been appreciated for some time that attention to literary forms is necessary to interpret texts. A similar attention to the forms of celebration and their complementarity to one another is necessary in interpreting liturgical texts and actions.

GOD'S ACTION

Catholic theology has justified the church's belief in the gracious efficacy of sacraments by the theory of divine institution. In the liturgy itself, the belief in God's presence and action is symbolized in the several ways in which its memorial character is expressed. The most obvious way is to repeat within the celebration the ordinance which sets it up as the commemoration of a particular historical event. In the Old Testament, the observance of the Sabbath, the Passover feast, the feast of Weeks, and the feast of Tents are all prescribed by ordinance,[10] so that the events of the Exodus may be duly remembered and celebrated from generation to generation. God's continuing presence with the people was guaranteed by the faithful observance of these ordinances. Jewish custom included a recital of these ordinances within the act of worship, either explicitly or by way of implicit reference.[11] Another way of expressing that the action was done in obedience to God's command to keep memory was to include prayers for the guarantee and acceptance of the cult, clearly implying that it is without ground unless given to the people by God and maintained by a divine presence. Thus the *Abodah* prayer of the synagogue *Tefillah* reads:

"Accept, JHWH, our God, thy people Israel and their prayer and restore the service to the Holy of Holies of thy house and receive speedily in love and favor the fire-offerings of Israel and their prayer, and may the service of thy people Israel ever be acceptable unto thee, and let our eyes behold thy return to Zion in mercy."[12]

Of course the most common way of expressing

worship's memorial character was to recite the account of the event remembered and to sing prayers and hymns which acknowledged God's continuing presence among the people and in worship, in the wake of that event. Although commentators have remarked on the sacerdotalizing tendencies of Israel's worship, it remains true that this historical character of Jewish worship made it different from the cosmic religions and cult which surrounded Israel.[13] God was deemed present in worship because of the presence of divine action in history.

These ways of expressing belief in the presence in worship of the God of history continue in modified form in Christian liturgy. The obvious case of reciting the ordinance that grounds the liturgy is the Supper narrative within the eucharistic prayer. Unfortunately this has been interpreted as an effective repetition of Christ's words for the transformation of the bread and wine into his body and blood. Its original purpose was to recall within the prayer a command and a basic format of prayer that has its ground in what Jesus did and said. In other words, its place and function in the prayer is to give a guarantee and an authority to the entire memorial action.[14]

Some early ordination prayers carry similar references to a divine action of institution. The prayer for the ordination of a bishop in the *Treatise on the Apostolic Tradition* addressing God recalls:

"thou . . . hast set bounds within the church through the word of thy grace, preordaining from the beginning the race of the just people of Abraham, establishing princes and priests and not leaving thy sanctuary without a ministry. . . ."[15]

Similar clauses occur in the prayer for the ordination of presbyters. The biblical reference is to the diffusion of the spirit of Moses over the seventy elders of Israel. In the prayer for the ordination of presbyters in the Verona Sacramentary, one finds the same reference to Moses and the elders and also one to Aaron and his sons. Aaron's consecration on the order of God to Moses is likewise recalled in that Sacramentary's prayer for the ordination of a bishop.[16] Tracing Christian ordination back to these biblical scenes is much more dubious than tracing the Supper back to Jesus Christ. However, the intent of the prayer is similar: liturgical action of its nature is based on a divine command.

In other instances, mention of a divine command or institution is not as explicit, but the same basic view appears, that things must be done according to a properly ordained way. In the prayer over the baptismal water, for example, a number of biblical events of both Old and New Testament are recalled as the ground for this blessing and for the baptismal ritual. In the blessing of the most recently revised Latin Rite, Christ's baptism in the Jordan and the water that flowed from his side when the centurion pierced it with his lance are recalled. These incidents are remembered as a kind of divine ordinance for the sacrament of baptism, without any literal intent of ascribing its institution to either of these moments. Blessings for other sacramental materials, such as the oil of anointing, and over people in marriage and penance have a similar moment of appeal to a biblical foundation. The intention of the prayers is always symbolic rather than legal. The significance of the motif is that the community finds the justification of its prayer and sacrament in the divine will that memorial should be kept in this way. This guarantees that God remains with the people and blesses them in their celebration.

In the Latin liturgy, the declaratory form, indicating an action done in the power of Christ, such as "I baptize you," took precedence over the prayer of blessing in which an ordinance symbol is included. This served the same purpose of asserting God's action, but in a legalistic way that refers more readily to an institution than to a historical event as the guarantee of efficacy. As liturgy is now being revised, more attention is being given to the place of prayers of blessing (both thanksgiving and supplication) in all sacraments and other liturgical actions. The result is somewhat schizophrenic, however, since both forms are retained and the rubrics give more moment to the declaratory forms than to the prayers. This residual legalism should not divert attention from the blessings, whether they be prescribed for validity or not. The meaning of sacrament is lost when the blessings are lost. The distinction between the *opus operatum* of the central priestly act and the accessory nature of other acts replaces the historical canon which points to the integrity and unity of the entire celebration. If we stay with the historical canon, and overcome the sacerdotalizing which overestimates the power of institution, we will note that liturgy is guaranteed by God's fidelity and testimony, which attached to the historical event and that now attaches to its liturgical remembrance. This is what liturgy signifies of itself when it is fully and duly celebrated.

TESTIMONY
In the analysis of faith that is a traditional part of Catholic theology, one theory states that the act of faith is an assent to God's testimony as such. That is, we do not assent to revelation because we believe in God, but faith is an assent to God and to the testimony at one and the same time. This is another way of saying that God and the historical act whereby revelation is given are so intertwined that God is knowable as Savior and Redeemer only in and through that act.[17] The testimony given in history is communicated to the church through the scriptures and their proclamation. The presence of

152

that same testimony in the liturgy is the ultimate reason why it is an act of God and an expression of the church's faith at one and the same time.

Proclaiming the scriptures in the liturgy is certainly one reason for saying that God's testimony is given in it. Added here is that the same testimony is attached to the ritual element of liturgy, to the sacramental actions of table-sharing, water immersion, anointing, and so forth. As already seen, the ritual action signifies the community, or ritualizes some particular activity of the community. In this same action, in virtue of metonymy, God's presence in Christ is signified as pure gift and as nonidentical with the church, and consequently as promise of the future. Therefore, the relation of God's testimony to the ritual action signifies two things which complete the testimony given in the word. The first of these is testimony to God's presence in this particular community, in fidelity to what has been done and promised by way of anticipation of the kingdom. Second, the ritual element adds to the word testimony about the *manner* of God's saving act and presence, precisely because of the symbolism of metonymy. In other words, God's presence among the Christian people, as other and as self-communicating in grace, is necessarily of the mode signified in sacrament. This is a presence of pure gift which is not to be identified either with the things in which this presence is disclosed or with the community which is itself signified in the action. God's gratuity and freedom are thus signified in ritual form in a way which complements the testimony given in the word about the gift of grace. Ritual's message is that all knowledge of the self must be gained by letting oneself be enlightened and judged by this event, that there is a limit to one's powers of self-healing and self-making, and that wholeness comes only by submitting to the forgiving and healing which is promised in Jesus Christ. Its message is also that human wisdom is folly, that society's or culture's claims

153

to total or absolute knowledge are a false ambition, and that the only true wisdom is that which is revealed in the cross of Jesus Christ. It is the appropriation of this testimony that liturgy both demands and makes possible.

TESTIMONY ABOUT JESUS CHRIST: THE ROOT-METAPHOR

God's testimony to Jesus Christ in the scriptural word and the testimony of Jesus to God in his "Abba" experience converge and coincide. The community does not have direct access to this experience, but comes to it through the word, which brings it to language, and through the testimony of those who live by this faith, especially those whose solidarity with Jesus in his suffering is most evident.

If the testimony given in word and sacrament about Jesus' death and resurrection constitutes the liturgy as both a divine action and a faith expression, then one must raise the issue of liturgy's root-metaphor. The root-metaphor is the key articulation of this "Abba" experience by which the meaning of other symbols is determined, or around which other symbols cluster. The issue is not simple, even though it is often repeated that the Pasch is the heart of the liturgy, or even that it is the root-metaphor. Since historically the Pasch has been articulated in divergent ways, the matter is not settled all that simply.

In any culture or symbol system, a root-metaphor resolves conflicts and makes life and death issues meaningful. It provides the core of a fuller construct. A root-metaphor may provide the core of all storytelling, as when the descent into Hades is used in Syriac literature as the focal point for the story of Christ's death. It may also provide the foundation for a system of thought, as when Anselm of Canterbury adopted from the penitential system the metaphor of satisfaction to build up an explanation of the value of Christ's death for our redemption. It may also serve as the key to a complex set of operations, as when passage becomes the metaphor both for understanding Christ's death and for the practice of Christian spirituality.

The history of the feast of the Pasch seems to have shed the most light on the root-metaphor for the memorial of Christ's mysteries in the liturgy. These historical studies also seem to shed light on other liturgical and sacramental practices. In effect, they point to two different understandings of Pasch, the one centering around the image "Pascha/Passio," the other around the image "Pascha/Transitus." These are two distinct root-metaphors, for the one centers attention on the passion itself, the other on the passage through death to life. The distinction gives rise to two different ways of keeping memorial and to two different ways of participating in life in the mystery remembered.[18]

The tradition which takes Pasch as passion points more explicitly to the suffering Lord and to his experience of God in that suffering. The resurrection symbolizes the victory of that death, of the victory of life in death itself. In Johannine terms, the hour of death is the hour of Jesus' glorification; glory is manifested on the cross and the cross is its symbol. The tradition which associates Pasch with passage understands the resurrection as the anti-pole of death. Jesus passes through death to life and to glory. The death is more the condition of glory than its manifestation; the victory is given in the raising up to life, not in the death itself.

The tradition which concentrates on the death or passion as God's victory in Christ over the powers of darkness and death seems to have been strongest in the early church. It is a way of celebrating Christ which is associated with a humbler church, one that is weak by human standards and in which the testimony of

155

martyr's blood was important. The nurturing role that the church assumed for its membership seems to explain at least partly the choice of the pattern of passage over that of triumph in death. We see how this view dominated as church leadership and liturgical patterns provided for the progressive conversion of members, catechumens, and baptized. It came into focus during the centuries when the catechumenate was highly organized and received many adult members. This view served well in later centuries also, when many baptized in childhood went through spiritual conversion through penance and through an ongoing participation in the eucharist, where they associated themselves with the satisfaction for sin that Christ offered in his passion and death. The starkness of the Johannine glory, given in death itself, may be difficult to assimilate for those who wage constant war against temptation and weakness, and who are more in the position of children seeking milk than of martyrs giving witness in their own lives to the death which they commemorate.

Proclaimed in this testimony[19] is that the meaning which transforms human reality and experience *can be* given only by God, *is* given by God, is given *freely* by God, and is given *in and through a particular history*. Absolute significance and promise are attached to one particular event, so that other events are significant by their relation to it.

In this testimony, there is a divine response to human seeking, at both its most meaningful and its most vulnerable. In the human quest for the ultimate there is a twofold urge, which can turn into a twofold claim. This urge and claim are to the immediacy of self-consciousness and knowledge and to absolute knowledge of all things. Cultures in their own way deal with this desire, and their success or failure depends largely on setting realistic limits to the claim, while at

156

the same time satisfying it in some measure. The immediacy of self-consciousness is an illusion, and this is implicit in the way cultures offer the possibility of knowledge of the human not through introspection but through the common fund of stories, traditions, and institutions. In our own day, the illusion of the immediacy of self-knowledge is pursued beyond limits, in the thought that continuing to probe the unconscious will eventually reveal the solution to all problems. Cultures also promise a certain wholeness of knowledge about reality, in the sense that their cultural systems seek to integrate all phenomena and to offer ultimate explanations. Their success in regulating human life may well depend on how they allow their vision to encompass mystery and to set limits to the claims of knowledge.

The testimony of God which presents Jesus Christ as the Alpha and the Omega is a response to this double quest. There must be a place in liturgy for metaphors of process and for holding out the hope of life after death, whether physical or spiritual. Nevertheless, it is appropriate—in view of present liturgical renewal and current ecclesial consciousness of the church's relation to human systems—to ask whether the time has come to look to the testimony of life and victory given in the death of Jesus. Much in current christology points to the importance of that theme in the scriptures and to an understanding of Jesus' Abba experience as one of trust and nonabandonment by God in the very hour of darkness. Jesus' testimony to God is given in his death, and God's testimony about Jesus is given in the message of the resurrection, which assures us that God did not abandon him in his death but remained in communion with him in his most vulnerable and weakest hour. Ecclesial consciousness today is aware of the many victims that human society, political and ecclesiastical, has created down through the centuries.

It more clearly understands Jesus' preaching and death as a witness against the false claims which are the source of turmoil and the instruments used to deny human freedom to many. The church recognizes that it may be in its own death, or in the death of its members, that its witness to God and to freedom may need to be given. It is fitting then that its liturgical commemoration of Jesus' death or Pasch centers around the root-metaphor of *Pascha/Passio*. This is the dangerous memory which arouses the church's own readiness to stand with victims and to give witness.

SYMBOL OF THE FATHER[20]
In referring to Jesus' "Abba" experience and the testimony to it in the passion narrative and other New Testament passages, we come to liturgy's invocation of God as Father. It is a confusing image for several reasons, but the very confusion indicates the conversion involved in getting inside symbolic language, where we are addressed by, and we ourselves address, God. At such a point it is impossible to take the divine names as so many images out of which to make a mosaic.

Some feel that God's fatherhood is a hard doctrine to teach because so many children have poor fathers. To them it can only be granted that if the child's own father is made the point of comparison for an illustration of divine paternity, then God becomes little better than a shopkeeper worried about the rent. The predication of paternity bothers others, since it is such a severely masculine and even patriarchal image. An immediate, if not very deep, response to such complaint points to the juxtaposition of images found in such a statement of doctrine as this: "We must believe that the Son was not made out of nothing, nor out of some substance or other, but *from the womb* [italics added] of the Father, that is that he was begotten or born from the Father's own being."[21] This shows that there is nothing exclusively masculine about the church's idea of Christ's relationship to God or about the divine being. It may be the church's patriarchy rather than God's word which renders the use of the symbol problematic. In any case, quite a difference exists between teaching doctrines and invoking God, and it is the invocation that now concerns us.

The truth is that "Abba" is an invocation whose meaning is not self-evident. Vergote deals with the problem by saying that "Father" is not a symbol at all, for "the point is that the term is not meant to signify but is part of the vocabulary of recognition."[22] This seems to confuse symbol with image, however, so it is better to recognize that using symbol is self-involving, and to speak with Ricoeur of the zero content of the *figure* "Father" and so of passing from the phantasm to the symbol of the Father.[23]

Many of the things already said about symbol are verified supremely in the case of this address, where God says: "Thou art my Son, this day I have begotten thee," and Jesus responds "Abba, Father." It is a symbol which has its roots deep in human experience, in both its archeological depths and its teleological desires. It is not a simple image, where we can pass easily in context from first to second meaning. It is more the sort of symbol which, like sacrifice, through conjunction with many images has picked up a rather complex signification. As in the growth and development of symbols, earlier meanings had to be broken and then integrated at a higher level as context demanded. It is a symbol where metaphor is also at work, for there is a transfer of name which is striking, and it is in the transfer that the symbolic meaning is given. The word cannot be heard nor the address made except by one who is prepared to face the conflict that arises from the metaphorical usage.

159

Jesus' use of the word in addressing God has to be considered against the background of the earlier use of the term in Israel's history and in the light of the new meaning attached to it by reason of its relationship to the cross in Jesus' experience. First, in comparison with the cosmic religions surrounding it, Israel showed a marked diffidence in designating God as father. Israel's prophetic religion wished to break with any idea that humanity was generated by a god or some supernatural being. Nevertheless, the term reentered its vocabulary in conjunction not with creation but with election. Calling God the father of the people meant that there was a special relation of Yahweh to Israel because of the covenant. The image of a new creation was used to refer to the divine choice. God's fatherhood in such a context did not take in all of humanity but only Israel. By and large, the designation had a transsexual content completed by mother images, as in Hosea 11:1–4.

The next step in the development was the replacement of the designation "father" by a marriage image, that of God and Israel as spouses. This new description occurs within the context of covenant, which completes the imagery of election. A mutual relation is demanded in which Israel has responsibility in the face of God and cannot simply look to God to cure all its ills, even when it is unfaithful. Within this context an *invocation* of God as father begins to replace the *designation* of God as father. It is an address used between lovers, significant of a convenantal relationship where the partners have responsibilities to one another.

The meaning signified in the New Testament takes up from this point, but again radically changes the invocation on several scores. On the lips of Jesus, the exclusivity of God's relation to Israel is abandoned. In his preaching and in his prayer to God, election and covenant extend to all humanity. It is an election which shows a predilection for the poor and simple (Mt 11). God's address to Jesus as Son clearly refers to his mission, and the key moment of Jesus' address to God as "Abba" is in the passion and on the cross. When Jesus teaches the disciples to pray to God as "Abba," the prayer is eschatological, one in which the hope and expectation of the kingdom that comes from Jesus' witness may be expressed. In the Pauline writings and in the letter to the Hebrews, the connection between the fatherhood of God and the cross is made explicit. Jesus enters into his sonship through his death, and the prayer of the Spirit in the heart of believers which prompts them to address God as "Abba" is a prayer made in participation of Jesus' death.

The biblical witness, taken up into the liturgy, makes it clear that the address to God as "Abba" refers to God's gratuitous election, with the covenant which requires a response from the people chosen, with the experience of God that Jesus had in the passion, and with the expectation of the coming kingdom. It also shows that in the symbol, images of mother and spouse complete the image of paternity. In liturgical invocation, therefore, context is all. Sometimes one hears the invocation "Mother" replacing that of "Father" in current prayer. That is quite legitimate, but it should not lead simply to a confusion of images. Always the key issue is the attitude and experience out of which God is being addressed and the context of language in which the address occurs. Does it express the relationship which is grounded in election, covenant, cross, and hope of the kingdom?

In the past few decades, a number of writers have made ample use of the Freudian analysis of the Oedipal complex to explicate the symbol of God the Father.[24] These reflections are too complex to adequately account for here. A very brief discussion will have to suffice to show that interiorization and a growth in relationship are bound up with use of the invocation.[25]

According to Freud, the rivalry between son and father is rooted in the son's desire to possess the life that he attributes to the father. He looks for identification with an idealized father, while at the same time he is unable to claim his own identity as long as this goes on. Therefore it is necessary to kill the idealized father. This original stage of the relationship has much to do with what the child expects from the father, but in which he is disappointed. It is also pointed out that both the complex and its analysis are determined by cultural conditions which determine the nature of family relations, so that the conflict is not properly rooted in masculinity, but instead has more to do with the actual position that the father has had in the Western family.

The conflict's resolution lies in mutual recognition of father and son, where difference and independence become the condition of the mutual relationship in the enjoyment of what they possess in common. The father gives the child an independent existence and responsibility together with recognition of this. To accept this recognition and relationship, the child must renounce the fantasies that spring from the initial desire to be one with an idealized father, to receive everything from him. The early relationship persists in a new way, however, inasmuch as mature mutual recognition requires an acknowledgment of boundedness and of what is possessed in common. Independence does not destroy similitude and the basis of friendship in oneness of flesh and inheritance.

It is suggested that the relationship with God develops according to a comparable pattern. There is an initial stage of wanting everything from God, of exaggerating God's providence and expecting the fulfillment of

162

undifferentiated and fantastic desires. Then comes a break and a stage of disappointment, indeed something of a hatred of God, which most people suppress and refuse to recognize out of fear, not realizing that they must break with a false image. This conflict is resolved when one hears God granting independent selfhood and a covenantal relationship, where one is invited to act out of the life and gifts that one possesses. The similitude within difference that remains the ground of this mature relationship is symbolized in the gift of the Spirit, which comes from God and resides within the person, the source of the address to God as "Abba."

An experience of abandonment by God is part of interiorizing the relationship signified in the address "Abba." Biblical revelation denies the Father of whom we expect everything and who questions our right to independence, responsibility, and free choice, and so in fact frustrates desire. Also denied is the Father of a mutual contract, which is the first fantasy with which we try to replace the other. The covenantal relationship must be worked out within the boundaries set to desire and independence by a mature person. The Father does not abandon those who experience the cross, in what relates to them personally and in what relates to their life for others, but requires that they recognize that life and hope are God's gifts and come according to the conditions of God's promise.

The cross stands at the heart of Jesus' relationship with God and of the relationship in which the church expresses its desire to participate in addressing God as "Father." While the cross is the pattern of human relationship with God, it is also the pattern for relationship with human persons and societies. In the crucifixion, Jesus stood firm in his solidarity with the marginal, the poor, and the oppressed. More and more we recognize that the friends and disciples of Jesus, those for whom he gave his life, were those to whom religious, political, and cultural institutions denied independence and the free possibilities for a full human existence. They were those to whom humanity denied the free gift of God. In this sense Jesus died so that human persons might be allowed those religious and cultural conditions necessary for a fully personal relationship with God. He died giving testimony for God and against any human construction which would curtail the gift of life that God gives in covenant and freedom. Paradoxically, the symbolism of Father is a contradiction of all that we associate with paternalism and patriarchy, totalitarianism and tyranny. Addressing God as "Abba" in the memorial of Jesus' death in worship involves us in the human enterprise which engages God's people in giving witness to the promise of the kingdom.

APPROPRIATION OF TESTIMONY:
LAMENTATION AND THANKSGIVING
Summarizing Paul Ricoeur, Lewis Mudge says of testimony that it:

". . . claims to be discourse in which, in a moment of total unity between event and meaning, an individual or community has found 'its effort to exist and desire to be' interpreted to the point of total dispossession or divestment of the claims of the self. Every attempt of the self to be source of meaning in its own right has yielded before the question, 'Who is God?'. And the event or combination of events in which this has happened has been interpreted as a 'trace' of the Absolute at this historical moment."[26]

Before such testimony there can only be divestment of self and self's claims, so that Ricouer himself writes of appropriation of the text in which the testimony is given:

"If the reference of the text is the project of a world, then it is not the reader who primarily projects himself.

The reader rather is enlarged in his capacity of self-projection by receiving a new mode of being. . . . Appropriation ceases to appear as a kind of possession, as a way of taking hold of things; instead it implies a moment of dispossession of the egoistic and narcissistic ego. . . ."[27]

Ricoeur's statement applies in a general sense to any text which offers a world of meaning to the reader, but he has made clear elsewhere how much more profound this kind of response is when we are faced with God's testimony in Jesus Christ. On the basis of these perceptions, it is now suggested that the church's liturgy is the consummate place and expression of the appropriation of scriptural testimony, which is then presented in the liturgical celebration itself. So far, we have talked about the ways in which this testimony is given. Now we can say that the specific way in which the church appropriates this testimony in liturgy is the prayer of lamentation and thanksgiving.[28] It is in these two ways that—in receiving and responding to God's testimony—the community's own experience and self-expression are formulated verbally and in the formulation transformed. They become the ground of that ethic and witness which is in turn expressed in the liturgy's ritual actions of shared table and care.

Lamentation expresses the community's perception of its own and of humanity's sin and of the shackles which are placed on human freedom and on God's word and gift. Griefs which have been suppressed and hopes which have been stilled are allowed expression. In this act, the community remembers the questions to which the gospel speaks instead of stilling them.

Lamentation played a considerable part in Israel's history, especially in the mouths of prophets. It brought the people to a sense of their own need, as well as to a sense of the forces which oppressed them and denied their freedom. The tribes would never have left Egypt

165

had they not found someone to articulate their woes and griefs and to stand with them in doing so, not before any human power but before the God of their forebears. The Israelite people would never have sought a return to the covenant and its messianic hopes in the period of the kingdom unless prophets had taught them to lament the shackles that kings and their sacral institutions put on them in the interests of more power and security, shackles that distorted their very worship. Those who were carried into exile would never have desired to return, or kept their identity in a place of exile, unless they had grieved over their separation from God who abode in Jerusalem. Even the political destiny promised to a faithful people by a faithful God could be envisaged only by those who sat and wept over Jerusalem, whether in its time of sin or in its time of ruin and slavery.

Chaos, senselessness, and meaninglessness are part and parcel of human experience. They can be so massive, so terrifying, that societies are built on the capacity to forget. It has been remarked often enough of our own age that senseless death is so daily, so much the fruit of our way of life, so imminent and so global, so prone to reduce thousands to a living death, that peoples ignore it and suppress its remembrance in what they choose to honor. Keeping memory of Jesus can make room for the expression of fears, terror, emptiness, and blindness, of the offense and the cruelty that mark our way of being and our social institutions.

Lamentation appropriates that part of God's testimony which questions the human claim to absolute knowledge and control and the human way of acting which forgets the poor and the needy. It is actually one aspect of expressing hope, for it is possible to recognize sin and sinfulness only where there is hope. In remembering Jesus, it is possible to acknowledge "that all human enactments require criticism, revision and reenactment—and that this process is within God."[29] The lament carries the seed of hope that the poor and desolate and all who live a shadowy existence will be vindicated. It is a lament of compassion, not empty moaning.

Lamentation leads to doxology because doxology engages us in the promise of newness that comes with the gift of the Spirit, who heals, unites, and empowers. That which is remembered in grief is redeemed, made whole, renewed. The community that grieves knows that God's power is not co-opted by human power structures, but that it is free and is the vital force behind the hope of the kingdom. Responding to a memorial narrative in which the promise engaged in the resurrection dominates the tale, the Christian people give voice to praise and thanksgiving. By engaging in this act, they strip themselves of all modes of discourse and expression that seek to control the sacred, that resort to power structures for the images of the divine name. Instead they turn to the history in which God is present, listen to the names that God assumes in this history and to the promises it contains. Praise and thanksgiving is the central act of worship because it flows from the recognition that by becoming one with the history proclaimed, by entering the world opened up by God's testimony, the community is transformed and becomes the dwelling place of God's Spirit. By appropriating the freedom of God, they themselves are set free.

In brief, lamentation and thanksgiving are the symbolic acts by which the community appropriates the name that God has assumed and the promises that have been made. They know no other name than this. The name is complex and multiple and derives some of its content from cosmic religions and hierophanies, but above all it is a name spoken in history and in promise. It is complex because of human desires and aspirations. In itself it is simple.

CONCLUSION

The starting point of this chapter's explanation of liturgy as an act of God and of the church was that it brings about a transformation of experience. The experience in question is not generic experience, however, but the particular experience of a community that lives by faith in Jesus Christ and by a gospel ethic, and has therefore a special sense of identity. Faith and moral action are the ground of liturgical celebration. In the second place, it was said that this transformation takes place through the work of the entire sacramental canon. Celebration includes all the forms of discourse that are pertinent to liturgy's meaning. Third, it was remarked that God's action in the liturgy was guaranteed traditionally by the notion of divine institution, but that this guarantee might well be explained in terms of the testimony given in liturgy to the significance of Jesus' death. This testimony is given both in word, especially in memorial narrative, and in ritual action, indicative of the manner of God's presence to the community that remembers. Fourth, it was said that the key to the understanding of this testimony about Jesus' death is the root-metaphor of *Pascha/Passio*. Fifth, it was shown how the invitation to address God as *Abba* completes the testimony in expressing the nature of the relationship to God given to us in Jesus Christ. Sixth, it was explained how in the sacramental canon this address takes on the forms of lamentation and thanksgiving, which then constitute the appropriation of the divine testimony regarding the death of Jesus and our regeneration through this death as God's children.

NOTES

1. Paul Ricoeur, *The Symbolism of Evil*, translated by Emerson Buchanan (Boston: Beacon Press, 1967), p. 350.

168

2. Thomas Torrance, *Theology in Reconciliation* (London: Chapman, 1975), pp. 139–214.

3. Basil of Caeserea, The Treatise *De Spiritu Sancto,* in *Nicene and Post-Nicene Fathers of the Christian Church,* vol. 8 (New York: Christian Literature, 1895), pp. 1–50.

4. Josef Jungmann, *The Place of Christ in Liturgical Prayer* (New York: Alba, 1965), pp. 186–87, 246–47.

5. Edward Schillebeeckx, *Christ the Sacrament of the Encounter with God,* translated by Cornelius Ernst (Kansas City: Sheed Andrews & McMeel, 1963).

6. Compare this with the definition given by Tad Guzie, *The Book of Sacramental Basics* (New York: Paulist Press, 1981), p. 53: "A sacrament is a festive action in which Christians assemble to celebrate their lived experience and to call to heart their common story. The action is a symbol of God's care for us in Christ. Enacting the symbol brings us closer to one another in the church and to the Lord who is there for us."

7. Charles Perrot, "L'eucharistie dans le Nouveau Testament," *La Maison-Dieu* 167:1 (1979), 109–25.

8. A good example is *Sermon LXXII, On the Lord's Resurrection II,* in *Nicene and Post-Nicene Fathers of the Christian Church,* vol. 7 (New York: Christian Literature, 1895), pp. 184–86.

9. Harvey H. Guthrie, *Theology as Thanksgiving: From Israel's Psalms to the Church's Eucharist* (New York: Seabury Press, 1981), pp. 181–216.

10. For a brief history of the origins of festivals, see Eckart Otto & Tim Schramm, *Festival and Joy* (Nashville: Abingdon Press, 1980).

11. On the relation of this to the eucharistic prayer see Louis Ligier, "The origins of the eucharistic prayer," *Studia Liturgica* 9 (1973), 161–85.

12. The text may be found in Louis Bouyer, *Eucharist: Theology and Spirituality of the Eucharistic Prayer* (Notre Dame, Ind.: University of Notre Dame Press, 1968), p. 132.

13. Erich Zenger, "Ritual and criticism of ritual in the Old Testament," *Concilium* 112 (New York: Seabury Press, 1979), pp. 39–49.

14. Edward Kilmartin, "Sacrificium laudis: Content and function of early eucharistic prayers," *Theological Studies* 35 (1974), 268–87.

15. Gregory Dix, *The Treatise on the Apostolic Tradition of St. Hippolytus of Rome*, reissued by Henry Chadwick (London: SPCK, 1968), pp. x–xx.

16. There is an English translation in H. B. Porter, *The Ordination Prayers of the Ancient Western Churches* (London: SPCK, 1967), p. 33.

17. Questions about the natural knowledge of God are deliberately avoided here.

18. On the early history of the Pasch, see Georg Kretschmar, "Christliches Pascha . . ."; im 2. Jahrhundert und die Ausbildung der Christlichen Theologie," *Recherches de Sciences Religieuses* 60 (1972), 287–323 and A. Scheer, "Is the Easter Vigil a rite of passage?" *Concilium* 112 (New York: Herder & Herder, 1979), pp. 50–62.

19. Paul Ricoeur, "The hermeneutics of testimony," in Lewis S. Mudge (ed.), *Essays on Biblical Hermeneutics* (Philadelphia: Fortress Press, 1980), pp. 119–54, and Mudge's introduction, pp. 1–40.

20. The literature is vast. Suffice to mention Robert Hamerton-Kelly, *God the Father: Theology and Patriarchy in the Teaching of Jesus* (Philadelphia: Fortress Press, 1979); Paul Ricoeur, "Fatherhood: From phantasm to symbol," in *The Conflict of Interpretations: Essays in Hermeneutics*, translated by Don Ihde (Evanston, Ill.: Northwestern University Press, 1974), pp. 468–97; Johann B. Metz & Edward Schillebeeckx (eds.), *God as Father? Concilium* 143 (New York: Seabury Press, 1981).

21. Council of Toledo, A.D. 675, DS 276.

22. Cited by Claude Geffré, "Father as the proper name of God," *Concilium* 143 (New York: Seabury Press, 1981), p. 48.

23. Ricoeur, "Fatherhood: From phantasm to symbol."

24. Besides Ricoeur, one could mention C. Duquoc, *Dieu Différent* (Paris: Cerf, 1977); J.-M. Pohier, *Au Nom du Père. Recherches Théologiques et Psychanalytiques* (Paris: Cerf, 1972); A. Vergote, *Interprétation du Langage Religieux* (Paris: Seuil, 1974).

25. See the summary in Hamerton-Kelly, pp. 1–19.

26. Mudge, introduction to *Essays on Biblical Hermeneutics*, p. 18.

27. Paul Ricoeur, *Interpretation Theory: Discourse and the Surplus of Meaning* (Forth Worth: Texas Christian University Press, 1976), p. 92.

28. On these two forms of prayer in relation to prophecy and history, see Walter Brueggemann, *The Prophetic Imagination* (Philadelphia: Fortress Press, 1980); Claus Westermann, *Praise and Lament in the Psalms* (Atlanta: John Knox Press, 1981).

29. Stephen Happel, "The structure of our utopian mitsein (life-together)," *Concilium* 123 (New York: Seabury Press, 1979), p. 101.

Chapter Seven

Interpretation: Critical and Explanatory

Symbols mediate between experience and reality,
between the subjective and the objective, and between
the cognitive and the affective. Through them human
experience is brought to expression and so to discovery.
Through them reality is presented to the human
community in its wholeness and as an ultimate unity.
Without symbols there would be neither affective
wholeness nor knowledge of the truth. Symbols defy
reduction to the conceptual and keep open the
possibility of multiple and developing meanings. Their
very richness and polysemy is also their risk. While
communities need to believe in what they express in
order to live by them and understand them, they need
also to interpret them. Because symbol systems grow
and develop, their use needs to be regarded critically.
They do not dispense one from thought, but give rise
to it and demand it.

While symbols enrich life and make it human, the
greatest difficulty in their interpretation lies in their
opaqueness. In three different ways, they express the
inscrutable. First, they plunge into the arché of the
unconscious, into that obscure world of feelings and
values where the person relates to the most deep-
seated needs and desires, and senses the seriousness of
a healthy relation to body and cosmos. Psychic
dynamism and intellectual wonder converge in one
person, in one basic drive where unity is created
through the imagination. Second, they are the only

possible language to confront and deal with human limits, those that come from bodiliness and finitude and those that come from sin. Symbols express the complexity of these limits, establish the boundaries between the limits of finitude and the boundedness of will that is sin or sin-prone, and allow for consent to the realities of the human condition in both its limits and in its possibilities of emancipation. Third, while expressing both fundamental drives and human limit, symbols dare to express a totality of meaning, to present to the human mind the ultimate and the transcendent. The imagination dares to speak beyond knowing. It presents the ultimate not as acquired but as desirable, not as attained but as attainable.

Since they shed light upon this triple obscurity, symbols need constant interpretation. More specific to Christian liturgy is the need to interpret its mediation of the gospel kerygma to a diversity of cultures and over a long period of history. Liturgical studies in recent times have shown more and more interest in Christian liturgy's roots in Jewish worship. So many of the images and forms of prayer used by the early Christian community were taken from Judaism. Because of this, their kerygmatic message and their disclosures of God's presence in Christ and in the community of his disciples must be distinguished from the cultural mode. This is made difficult because Judaism in early Christian times was marked already by an encounter between Jewish and Hellenic cultures, and also because the New Testament books in some measure already show the effort to present Jesus Christ to non-Judaic cultures. As the acculturation of worship proceeded beyond New Testament times into the present era, symbols and forms of expression from a variety of cultures accumulated. Liturgy plays a basic role in making Jesus Christ and the gospel present to many peoples, and in opening up the symbolic expression of diverse cultures to an appropriation of this truth. On

173

the other hand, liturgy itself needs a mediator with the culture. This mediator is theological reflection, both critical and expository. The Christian community believes in both the apostolicity and the catholicity of its worship. That is, it professes to worship God in a way whose foundation is laid by the apostolic tradition, and it professes to allow communities in all times and in all places to acknowledge the one Redeemer and the one God. This common meaning across time and space can be mediated only by an interpretation which incorporates a dialectic between particular traditions and between diverse forms of expression. Ecumenically, reflecting upon the liturgical usages of churches can enable congregations to find both their common faith and their principal points of divergence, divergences which have both practical and speculative characteristics.

CRITICAL REFLECTION

Any kind of comprehensive theological presentation of liturgy and its meaning must be preceded by a critical consideration of liturgical traditions and practices. A critical sense is necessary if the gospel is to be truly free in its address to the churches and if people are to be free to listen to it, as well as free to allow for ongoing development. A kind of general principle is at work in the midst of such critical reflection which has to do with the nonidentity of the Word with any form in which it is spoken and of the Spirit with any voice in which it speaks. The absolute cannot be identified with any human culture, prayer, or institution. This is proclaimed in the historical events where traces of the absolute are found. Worship in its very listening to God functions as a critique of life and culture. It is the fitting place to struggle for freedom to hear the Word and let the Spirit speak. Some form of iconoclasm is inherent to every development of liturgical forms and to every community's or person's appropriation of its most basic modes. There is a necessary place for disillusionment in worship, a need for the readiness to face a restructuring of life, even while keeping the commonsense attitude which allows consent to the limits within which people live and from within which they continue to aspire to the fullness of the true and the good, to the fullness of communion with God and with one another in God.

Critical liturgiology attends to five factors in examining sacramental traditions and current celebrations, five things which inhibit freedom of the gospel and its appropriation, or inhibit the capacity of symbols to express the poetry of human relations. They are (1) naive realism, (2) turning symbols to allegorical purposes, (3) rationalizing symbols, (4) distorting symbol systems to support ideologies, and (5) the breakdown of communications within the symbolic world which leaves some, even many, lives semantically empty.

Naive Realism
Naive realism is bound up with the confusion between what is perceived and what is real or meaningful. It is principally an inflation of the visual element in symbol and a refusal of that interiority which is necessary to appropriate the verbal.[1] It confuses reality with what is seen, or stays at that stage of human development where what is seen is what is true. One odd thing about this is that fantasy quickly supplies what is not seen with the eyes, pretending to a perception of the hidden behind the apparent. Certain periods of liturgical history were particularly notable for this fascination with the visual, a fascination much influenced by the word becoming a closed book, a sacral language that was the preserve of the clergy (and sometimes not well understood by them). Under these circumstances all forms of the visual become extremely important. Belief in the visual is the test of faith.

Doubting communicants are confirmed in their faith by blood dripping from hosts, and processions and exposition of the blessed sacrament replace the primacy of the table and the gospel. Relics are put on display and carried around, and the exuberance of external decor in places of worship grows and grows.[2]

The austerity of the most recent liturgical renewal in Western churches has greatly curbed this visual factor, but has done so almost to the point of denying its real and continuing place within the sacramental system. As a result, some hanker after the fading aura of the sacred in places and acts of worship, and inevitably tend to return to the old. Some congregations or pastors have never forsaken the old, of course, and there are churches where the tinkling of bells at the institution narrative has never ceased to be heard, so that people may continue to look up in pious wonder. The clue to properly integrating the visual, however, is found in the things and actions that are made to command attention and with how they are attuned with the word that is spoken. It is enough to recall here what has already been said about the kind of ritual action that Christianity adopts and its concentration on the simplicity of the domestic. In effect, the attention and reverence with which a minister pours wine into the cup is more genuinely evangelical than displaying the host in a monstrance. The visual which attracts attention to what is to be eaten is different from the visual which displays what is not eaten.

Allegorization
Allegorization has two forms, one crude, the other sophisticated. In both cases, it neglects what is seen and said in favor of what is thought or imagined. It turns every word and every visible thing into an instruction or message. The sophisticated form is found in writers such as Origen who give a spiritual interpretation to all things, inspired as they are by some

kind of neo-Platonism.[3] The crude form is found in writings such as the exposition of the Mass, where anything can be made to represent whatever the expositor chooses. When the priest washes his hands after the presentation of gifts in the Mass, the people may be told that this represents Pilate. At Easter Vespers the deacons who sing the antiphons take on the role of the angels at the tomb.[4] While this sort of thing is associated with the medieval, it is not totally out of vogue. There was a stage in the recent liturgical movement when it seemed right and proper to supply allegorical meanings for the celebrant's vestments. Allegorization, for all its concentration on the visual in this cruder form, is in fact a neglect of the world of the senses, since it does not take them seriously in what they themselves perceive and express. One hopes that the day is gone or going when the cosmic imagery of light and darkness at Easter is so covered over by explanations of what the candle represents in the story of the Jews or of Christ that the candle itself is hardly noticed. Some of these allegorical explanations are woven deeply into theology, with serious consequences, as when the representation of Christ's death is so much read into the distinct consecration of bread and wine that the holy communion is neglected, and in conjunction with this, the community symbols are subordinated completely to the priestly presidency and action.[5]

Rationalization
Rationalization of symbols is their reduction to a conceptual content.[6] It claims more knowledge and understanding than is actually possessed, or even given in the symbols. Rationalization occurs in the passage from verbal symbols to conceptual symbols. Concepts such as original sin, transubstantiation, causality, and institution have a role to play in explaining liturgical mysteries. However, they can be overworked and allowed to substitute for images such as the story of

177

Adam, the presence of the Lord in the sacramental supper, the divine action of grace, and the liturgy's continuity with the apostolic tradition. Such concepts become symbols in their own right and stand to explain or present far more than they are able to carry. When the content of the verbal symbols is reduced to these concepts, the possibilities of both interpretation and celebration are limited severely.

Support for Ideology
A symbol system supports an ideology in the pejorative sense when it is used to uphold a given distribution of power and to justify such distribution as unconditionally necessary. Christian communities need their structures, their ministries, and their offices, but the current organization in the churches of the Roman patriarchate has become stabilized and sacralized beyond necessity. The manner of celebration has been given a divine quality that is illusionary.

The power structure becomes dangerous when it is innocently, uncritically, and rather literally accepted as of divine institution, so that the power of God is identified with the power of the ordained ministry. At the very moment when we say that the sacraments reveal and make present the power of God, we cannot but be struck by procedures which prevent some Christian fellowships from celebrating these same sacraments, or by structures wherein the female voice is forever silent. Have the very structures which the church has adopted to commemorate the gracious presence of God become the veil whereby the power that is a force for utopian vision is hidden from sight?

Today, alternative models of community organization and liturgical celebration are emerging which symbolize a different perception of God's presence in the church and in the world. Basic Christian communities allow for a more divergent ministry and often express a more politically conscious sense of God's action in human affairs. In a number of communities women take a prominent, and even a presidential, ministerial role. Such experiences are often marginal to hierarchical structures, and one cannot suggest at this stage that they have faced all the problems of meaning that they suggest implicitly. By and large, however, they are an imaginative exploration of the Christian symbol system. On the one hand they are diagnostic of what is ideological in the established system, and on the other they are suggestive of new possibilities.[7]

Semantically Empty Lives
The other side of this sacralization of certain types of power in the church is that it leaves many lives semantically empty. Instead of representing community and the power of God active in the people, symbols of power and ministry have been diverted to the priesthood and hierarchy, whose activity alone they express. Articulation of other gifts and services within the community or in the apostolate is then silenced. Again, this is one area where communities are becoming more conscious, although the old system can have such a strong hold that a kind of conflict of rituals results.

Furthermore, if symbolic liturgy is to give meaningful expression to all human experience, it needs to encompass the suffering and the marginal, to give voice to their liberation and to their place in God's kingdom. Expressing what Victor Turner[8] calls *communitas* and antistructure in the life of the church and in its presentation of the gospel of the kingdom is vital. *Communitas* is what is most basic to a shared life. It is more fundamental than the distribution of power and the organizations which belong to structure. One way to symbolize *communitas* is in ritual which can be styled antistructural. This is ritual wherein one's community role is subverted in order to point to that which is below structure, to that in which all are equal and which, at the same time, is the most important thing in the life of the group. When giving examples of this in Catholic liturgy, Turner points to what is most cosmic and ahistorical, such as the moment of consecration in the Mass where all bow in wonder and reverence before this spatial symbol of the sacred.[9] Therefore, one can agree with him on the importance of symbols of *communitas*, but disagree on where he finds them in liturgy and with the ahistorical perception he has of sacrament and of the holy. Symbolizing the power of the weak and recalling in memorial victims and those who live in solidarity with them, or have in the past done so, constitutes the vital force of *communitas* that is the presage of the kingdom.[10]

Critical attention to these five limitations on liturgical expression and interpretation is necessary in promoting positive fullness of language. Each of these trends puts some restriction on this fullness, leaves out some aspect of human experience, leaves out people, or prevents symbols from showing their full range of signification. An interpretation or model of celebration may be deemed inauthentic if it fails to address important features of human experience, if it identifies God's revelation with a system, or if it no longer allows the word to be heard as both prophetically critical of the present and as hopeful for the future.

ONTOLOGY OF SYMBOLS
Beyond the explanation of individual symbols and the symbolic process are the questions of ontology and of a comprehensive explanation of the world opened up by liturgical symbolism. Is it possible to explain symbol's relation to the transcendent and to speak of the world of Christian symbolism as a revelation of being?

The classical model of sacramental theory in scholastic theology approached sacrament primarily as a means of grace, or more technically as an instrumental cause of grace. Sacraments were explained as actions of Christ through the ordained priest, resulting in a transformation of the human person through grace and an ontological union with Christ. It was important to explain the mode of Christ's presence and action in the sacraments. Since it was necessary to explain how a material instrument could produce a spiritual effect, various theories were proposed, some of which savored of occasionalism, as though sacrament were no more than the occasion on which God conferred grace. Even more metaphysical theories did little to explain the relation between the sign-value of sacraments and their causal efficacy, except inasmuch as the signs were deemed to give knowledge about what was being done.

Early in the twentieth century, Louis Billot and Anscar Vonier[11] attempted to bring together the functions of sign and cause within the classical model by highlighting the principle that "sacraments cause what they signify," or "sacraments cause by signifying." This led to a greater attention to the sacramental signs themselves in doing theology and in discussing grace and the presence of Christ. Most valuable was the realization that Thomas Aquinas had intended to explain sacraments as signs. His analogies with the distinction between substance and accident, matter and form, and the like, were not intended to replace the primary appreciation of sign. It was because sacraments are signs that Aquinas found their place in the world of Christian revelation and economy, since as signs they have a threefold signification, namely, commemorative, representative, and prognostic. In other words, as signs, sacraments unite the past which they commemorate, the future toward which they point, and the present wherein they signify the operation of divine grace.

Much of Catholic theology, especially of the type which exhausted itself in minute examination of magisterial definitions, actually lost sight of some important elements in the scholastic tradition as shaped by Aquinas or Bonaventure. Three such elements in particular come to mind which were important to the ontology of the sacramental. The first is the integration of the way of negation alongside the way of affirmation and analogy. This set limits to every explanation, allowing for the nonidentity of God and God's grace with any theory or any institution. The second element is that analogies which treat of the divine must be based in human experience and in an understanding of human experience. Aquinas' psychological analogy to explain the mystery of the trinity was not purely conceptual, but was presented for those who could grasp from experience the process of human cognition and love. The analogy which adopted satisfaction as a mode to explain redemption had its source in penitential practice and in the sense of God that it reflected and communicated.[12] Analogies explaining the presence of Christ's body and blood in the eucharist presupposed that the reader was able to grasp the difference between seeing and understanding.

Even more important for sacramental theory was that the scholastic theory of causality included the notion of participation. Aquinas recognized the difficulty in using a common way of speaking of God and creatures. At the same time, he did not want to empty language of all significance by denying the possibility of some transfer of concepts and meanings from the human to the divine. The ontology of participation provided a basis for analogical discourse, that is, the understanding that the created partakes of the being of the creator. However, this implied an exemplarity which must not be allowed to slip into a univocity of speech. One may say that creatures imitate the divine, but one may not speak in the reverse order, comparing God to creatures. Participation does not imply the possession of any common form by both God and creatures. For example, the divine names are not a transfer from human experience of the form of being that the same names may imply in creatures. Hence in addition to participation and the exemplarity which it implies, analogical discourse must also take the foundation of efficient causality. In this way, perfections are predicated of God as efficient cause or as origin.

Thus in offering any theological theory, including an explanation of sacraments, Aquinas could be said to have set up a threefold task. First, creatures participate in God but this must be spoken of in a way that avoids all univocity. Second, in explaining the relation of creature to creator, theories must respect the distance between the infinite and the finite and therefore include negation. Third, this distance is to be spoken of in a way that avoids spatial connotation and so maintains the immanence of God in creation. As this threefold task applies to sacramental theory, it means that, in what they signify, sacraments represent a world in which human persons participate in the life of God and a world in which God is immanent. With these factors in mind, the model of efficient causality could not be conceived as an operation of one being upon another within a spatial sphere, or as an operation involving beings living in independent spheres and having to cross from one to another in order to act upon each other.

With this appreciation of the scholastic, we can move from a symbolic world conceived hierarchically to a world which in contemporary idiom is conceived more historically and is less committed to the hierarchy of being among creatures and agents already mentioned in earlier chapters. Two kinds of question need to be addressed in an ontology of sacraments and related to this perception of reality. One is their place in the human person's and human community's aspiration to the transcendent. The other is an explanation of the world and the divine which is disclosed in the liturgy.

This is a world in which God regenerates humanity, in which the superabundance of the gracious exceeds the abundance of the sinful, in which the holy is made manifest in the ordinary, and in which the utopia of the kingdom is anticipated. It is a world in which the word of God is addressed to the mythopoetic core of human person and so constitutes a divine self-communication. How does one speak ontologically of that world without being unfaithful to the mythopoetic mode of revelation?

THE SYMBOLIC AND THE HUMAN

Symbols have been described as an articulation and transformation of human experience. The various ways in which the symbolic addresses the complexity and profundity of human experience have been discussed. The ontological issue of the symbolic in Christian practice could be put in the terms Ray Hart uses in addressing the ontology of revelation:

"It worries the point of revelation's insertion in man's being and reality-sense. For example: if the revelation-tradition says, in one of its modes of saying, that man is 'new' in Jesus Christ, it remains to say this new man eventfully; it is still the problem of *logos*, of bringing the dynamics of manhood to a speech in which man can recognize himself."[13]

When we relate this question to liturgy we ask, what does it do to bring about this newness? Where does it fit into human articulation and experience so as to be the transformative power of God's word? What does it do to change humanity's relation to the world, affect its sense of history, and relate it to a vision of divine transcendence and loving gift?

In asking this question about symbol's insertion into reality sense, we must recognize that neither the perceiving subject nor the perceived object are what they appear to be in the immediacy of perception. The person has the impression of seeing clearly, of acting in freedom, of being self-conscious. The world that the person perceives, or the world represented to the person, is portrayed in images and impressions that carry the illusion of complete reality. Thus one is always tempted in liturgical celebration to be supremely confident about one's feelings and to rest with the immediacy of experience. One may thus feel that one has found both the self and a world in which to live.

The Christian liturgy, however, does not permit such quiescence. If fully attended to, its complex use of images and of modes of representation and discourse destroys the illusion of immediacy. Instead of allowing participants to indulge their illusions, it invites them to appropriate the world that it opens up through a process of destructuring and refashioning of meanings. In going through this process, one receives the gift of self that God offers. One comes to recognize one's illusions of freedom and lack of freedom and to receive an image of self which is none other than that of Jesus Christ. One renounces the desire for false autonomy in opening oneself to gift.

Four movements are involved in symbol's way of changing human perspective. The first brings us from a perception of persons and things as objects around us to a perception of the meaning with which they are endowed, at least potentially. The second movement necessarily follows upon this and brings us from a consideration of life in utilitarian terms to a grasp of values, values which are bound up with the relational. A third process leads from a search for outer signs of presence, meaning, and reality to a point where reality and meaning are constituted by an inner word and perception and by sharing in this interiority. The fourth process takes us from a world suffused with images that beat upon our senses to a world in which we dare to be imaginative and to explore reality by imaginative creativity. Understanding this fourfold process has vast consequences for an understanding and celebration of liturgy.

From Objects to Meaning

The first transition is from facts or objects to meaning, or from data to significance. The data or facts of liturgy are the signs, words, and actions used. They have a first and immediate referent in the data and things of life, such as sharing bread and wine, meeting together in a place, fearing the blemish of alienation, being sick, uniting together in wedlock, and the like. Their second referent in the world of revelation can also be spoken of in a first instance as data and things. This is the case when one is caught up in the physical reality of eating and drinking the body and blood, getting absolution from the priest, or wondering about how the spatiotemporal reality of Christ's death can be reenacted in liturgy in another time and place. One seeks reassurances at this level of expression and perception, reassurances that appeal to the physical. Are we really guaranteed that the bread and wine have been changed into physical realities of body and blood? Is forgiveness of sin guaranteed by the sign of priestly absolution, even if it be necessary to resort to an act of general absolution? Does the sacrament of anointing contain a promise of physical healing?

Liturgical symbolism, when celebrated with respect for its fullness of language, invites participants to move away from these kinds of questions and preoccupations. It invites us to place the presence of the body and blood within a context of a gathering of faith, to relate it to memorial narrative and thanksgiving, to find in it a promise of the future. It invites us to place the priestly power of forgiveness within a context of personal conversion and community reconciliation, to relate the promises of the sacrament of anointing to questions of faith and hope in the lordship of Jesus over creation. This transfer from facts to meaning carries its own reassurances, but they are those given to people overcome with the overpowering sense of God's love and startled by the significance of a world in which the memory of Jesus Christ and of his solidarity with the suffering and abandoned is the key force.

Many theological questions about sacraments are themselves grasped differently when one realizes that they are set in a world in which significance and meaning count, rather than a world of physical data divorced from further issues of meaning. A good example is found in recent debates about the doctrine of transubstantiation, a doctrine which to some seems threatened when theologians speak about sign and presence and use terms such as transsignification or symbolizification. The fear is that if primacy is given to sign and signified, it will no longer be given to reality. However, the idea of substantial change was itself used as an analogy to move from the physical world to the world of the signified. It implies no physical change, and metaphysical change is not understood by making it look like physical change. Instead, the analogy says that in the metaphysical world known through signs, or in the world of the signified, a change occurs which can be compared to the *process* of change in a world of physical things. Hence, the emphasis today on participating in the real world of the sacramental by perception of meaning is not alien to the original analogy. Still the caution must be stated that meaning as perceived is not necessarily the last word on the ontological issue. It tells us how humans enter the world of the ultimately real, but not necessarily what that reality is. This anticipates the second type of ontological question, mentioned earlier.

This quest for meaning instead of mere facts is of its nature a quest for unity. When instead of defining objects in categories we look for their meaning, we are on that religious quest for ultimate oneness. Many people gather together for worship, people of different age groups, social belonging, and even different cultures. Many words are spoken and many actions performed. If each of these persons, words, and actions is defined and separated from the others by reason of its special category, we have a multiplicity of objects connected only spatially and temporally. Religious symbolism, in pointing to the transcendent and to ultimate meaning, offers the point of unity where all things are consummated. Persons and communities conquer the fear of individual or corporate death when they no longer seek to maintain selfhood and individuality, but are ready to foretaste birth to new life in the experience of death.

From Utilitarianism to Values
The second process in which symbolic language engages the Christian community is a turn from a view of life that looks for the useful to an appreciation of the values disclosed in the symbols. Earlier in this work, it was mentioned that contemporary Western culture is organized largely on the basis of a mechanistic model which offers productivity and organization as goal and means. In some ways, sacramental usage anticipated this approach to the world by accenting the idea that sacraments are means of grace and by suffocating attention to the nature and reality of the things and words constituting the symbolic. Symbols put values into relief, however, and require awe and reverence for the things which signify, as a condition for the grasp of what is signified. The values signified as inherent to Christian faith are strangely contrary to the utilitarian, so that the morality of human action is seen not so much as pursuing goals but as abiding by values. These values are represented to the senses and imagination in the blessedness of the

poor and meek, in the service rendered in washing feet, in the opening of table-sharing in ways that defy the boundaries of kinship and society, in the narrative of the Lord's passion, and in the memory of the persecuted. However much Christians engage in an ethics of responsibility, in the human effort to build a just and peaceful society by establishing order, their acts of worship remind them of the values that lie at the heart of God's justice. They are prompted to give primacy to compassion and to include in pride of place the weak, the suffering, the handicapped, the humanly useless. Believers find divine revelation in what from a useful perspective is viewed as failure.

By including the material—especially by accentuating the wonder and beauty of simple things such as bread and water, tables and jugs—liturgy espouses ways of relating to the earth itself which forbid us to make the use of anything material a pure means to an end. Nothing can be integrated into life until it is held in awe and reverence. Humanity's dwelling on earth is a dwelling with things, not a dwelling won at the expense of their exploitation.

From External to the Inner Word
Symbols also bid their hearers and speakers to move from the babel of external words and commands to the silence of an inner word. When internal desires and conflicts are simply projected onto images outside of oneself, the inner word itself unfortunately is represented as an outer word, as something foisted upon one by alien forces. Only those who have interiorized the meaning of symbols to the point that the symbols become an inner creative force can communicate together in faith. Believing doctrines without question, obeying external commands, and performing prescribed rituals with exactitude may hold off chaos, protect a semblance of social coherence, and

keep a group from tumbling into the fury of conflicting desires and notions, but this kind of being together does not lead to communion, nor does it call on personal responsibility and the richness of many gifts. The words and signs of worship are ways in which meaning and love are expressed and shared. They are not the agents of external actions and ordered obedience, nor the signs of "out there" things of a world in which we are encaptured. They represent reciprocal presence in shared meaning, shared love, and shared life, and disclose a divine presence of Spirit at the heart of this communal life.

From Image to Imaginative
The transition from image to the imaginative encompasses the other three processes. Isolated images, whether visual or verbal, represent a small part of human experience, often a chaotic or bewildering part, often a desirable and affirmative part. When they are not related to one another properly within a pattern, they are a jumble and create a jumble of fears, attractions, and emotions. The creative force of imagination, especially one that plays with metaphor, is needed to bring order and finality to the complex experience figured in the multiplicity of images. One can always try to put images together like building blocks, but this is a refusal to probe their polysemy and vitality and to resolve in some creative way their apparent conflicts. This approach remains with data, with the purely useful, with what is outside one's own creative force. The imaginative is the unifying factor, that which presents a storied and ritualized world in which meaning prevails over data, value over utility, and the inner voice of the Spirit over all that assails us by way of human direction or human coercion. The imaginative frees us from dark forces of alienation in which the human itself is submerged.

190

To see the fourth process as inclusive of the first three is to see what is occurring in the concrete use and interpretation of symbolic language. In an earlier chapter, we saw that verbal images express elements and levels of human experience in a progressive pattern. One image can actually embrace another by breaking with an earlier meaning and assimilating the residual meaning into a new perspective. This is the work of imagination, which is ever questing for new meaning on the basis of meanings perceived previously but now broken with. Thus sin assimilated the residual meaning of blemish, and guilt the residual meaning of both sin and blemish. The process is never finished once and for all, but is always going on. In the eucharist, early Christians came together as God's elect, believing themselves to be the inheritance of Israel, but the notion of particular election had to be broken to include members of all races. The church for many centuries absorbed the notion of the history of the elect into a vision of two kingdoms and two cities and a distinction between sacred history and profane history. Only quite recently is there a move to assimilate this into an image of God's presence in history without distinction. The image of the elect was assimilated into the image of the city of God or God's kingdom, and this is now being assimilated into an image of God's reign in the transformation of human history.

This process of imaginative representation requires a break with data. In the example of sin, one must break with the mere fact of the troubled arché of the soul in order to set this mood in the context of broken relations, and to break with the lonely lament for broken relations in order to set it in the context of interpersonal responsibility and vicarious expiation. In the example of election, one must break with the fact of the existence of one particular people in order to include all the elect without numbering or distinguishing, and to break with the image of a world divided between citizens of two kingdoms in order to set the combat between powers into the context of total history.

Imaginative representation also requires a break with ways of estimation. For example, ritual is not reducible to the ordering of life by taboo and purification. It becomes a memorial of God's choice of a people, and then in the third stage of imagination, an openness to the perception of God's presence in all suffering and in all solidarity with suffering. This means a significant change in the basis on which relations and actions are founded, even among those who profess to pursue a good moral life. In the example of the eucharist as celebration of God's people, the estimation of persons cannot be based on the fact of being Jew or non-Jew, baptized or unbaptized, but must extend to encompass more people and other values to the degree that God's love and choice of the weak becomes one's own vision.

When the imagination forces the break with data and with what appears useful, it forces a break with all external circumscriptions of meaning and value. Instead of counting God's people, one sees all history in the image of God's love. Instead of using ritual to delimit the domain of relations and relations within this domain, one celebrates in it universal love. This is the language of the heart.

This fourfold movement wrought by fidelity to the fullness of symbolic language in liturgy converges on a sense of "otherness." This is true in a threefold way. First, it is a condition of human self-knowledge and human communication that one express oneself and one's own experience as "other" to the undifferentiated and chaotic world which is one's initial self-consciousness. It is only through communion in a culture and with a culture that people find the possibilities of genuine self-possession. This means seeing oneself as "other" within the otherness of culture. Second, symbols draw us into communion with others, others that are persons and traditions and communities. They reveal to us that life is lived in fullness only by those who risk this communion and who learn to perceive the reality of sharing within the differentiations that exist. Because of otherness, presence always involves an element of absence, and this is integrated into the very nature of symbolic representation. Third, religious symbol refers to ultimate reality as totally other. The presence of the divine in the world and to the world requires, as already explained earlier, the acknowledgment of difference, of nonidentity with the ways, persons, and things that represent that presence. Being in love without measure means being ready to be caught up into this quest for the other in a total self-renunciation, leaving behind whatever is alien to the call that is followed. The experience of the transcendent as articulated and made accessible through symbol points to a world in which meaning, value, and word attain their end in a final stillness where we are caught up into what is totally other to all that we have known and desired.

Before passing on to the second ontological question, it may be noted that inserting symbol into the human process results from the interplay of all the elements in the liturgical celebration. The sensorial, the ritual action, the verbal images, the mythos, and the doxology act upon one another so that together they bring about the fourfold transformation described. Putting things in schematic form risks impoverishment. Nonetheless, the schema given here may help reflection. First it outlines the process in general, and then gives one example to make it more concrete.

Pattern	*Example*
Experience	Sickness
↓	
Sensorial	Oil
↓	↓
Ritual action	Anointing in community
↓	↓
Verbal	
Image	Exorcism/healing/strength
Mythos	Gospel healings/passion
Doxology	Blessing of oil
	Prayer over sick
↓	↓
Transformation	
Facts to meaning	Raised up in faith
Utility to value	Compassion, witness
Outer to inner	Spirit confirms
Image to imaginative	Martyrs, kings, etc.

The example chosen is the experience of sickness, one in which both the sick person and all related to him or her feel the constraints of human limitation and dark forebodings of fault and guilt. The sensorial element used in the liturgy is oil, which comes from the earth and which has nourishing and soothing powers. It is used in a ritual action of anointing within a community which owns the sick person as a member and which acts with concern. Thus the community's general interest in the sick person's welfare is ritualized in the anointing. The verbal images which the liturgy associates with the anointing, to mention at least some prevalent ones, are exorcism, healing, and strength. Exorcism expresses the alienation from earth and life forces which a community feels in face of sickness and the sense of an evil which takes possession of life, partly from outside the community and partly due to its own fault. Healing expresses the desire for good health, for a return to normalcy, for an overcoming of the evil forces that inhibit life. Strength expresses the ability to combat and withstand all evil. Included here are the three levels of experience of sin mentioned in an earlier chapter: the deep feeling of blemish and alienation, the sense of relationships broken and the counterpart of healing, and the sense of assuming personal stance in face of what life brings. Out of the many readings found in the Lectionary for the anointing of the sick, the two categories here chosen are the gospel stories of healing and the passion narrative. These represent the mythos to which the experience and verbal images are related. They highlight by way of a representation of Christian conduct the incorporation of the sick person into the mystery of the Lord's passion and the belief in Jesus as Savior and Lord. The appropriation of what is proclaimed and promised in this manifold representation of God's presence to the sick person and to the community occurs in the blessing of the oil and the prayer over the sick person. The transformation which this symbolic action brings to the sick person and to the community can be explicated on the basis of the fourfold movement described in this chapter. Instead of staying with the facts of physical illness and cure, the believer comes to understand that God's response is to raise up the person through faith in Jesus Christ, and that this has no direct bearing on physical cure. One then grasps the values within a Christian approach to illness, especially those of compassion and martyrion, that is to say, giving testimony to the Lord in weakness. This comes about not on the basis of external solace and encouragement, but only when the external is appropriated in such a way as to constitute an inner force, to put one in touch with the indwelling Spirit. Finally, rather than staying with the images of exorcism or healing or nourishment, the liturgy engages in the kind of imaginative discourse which relates the experience of a sick person to the stories of kings,

prophets, and martyrs, and especially to that of Jesus
Christ.

GOD'S PRESENCE AND ACTION

The first half of the ontological question treats of how
the symbol inserts itself into the human person's quest
for the transcendent, so that it belongs to the very
constitution of person and community. Since theology
takes the liturgy as a divine action, the symbolic
constitution of the person in grace must be explained
on God's side as well. Since sacrament is God made
present to humanity in Jesus Christ, is it possible to
present any analogies which explain this divine self-
communication?

The issue is complex and overruns the scope of a
sacramental theology. Here it will be enough to outline
briefly some current approaches in Catholic theology
which relate to the issue of symbolic crisis outlined in
the first chapter.

It has already been seen that Catholic theology prior to
the midpoint of the present century was concerned
mostly with explaining the efficient causality of
sacraments. In doing so, it scarcely referred to the rest
of the liturgy, except in passing theories about the *opus
operantis ecclesiae*. This position has been irrevocably
changed by the writings of some major theologians,
especially Edward Schillebeeckx and Karl Rahner.[14]
These two theologians, each in his own way, developed
a theory which is referred to generally as symbolic
causality. This theory moves away from the category of
efficient causality to that of divine self-communication
through symbol. The nature of sacrament as sign is
thus made the core of its explanation, and the notion of
sacrament is broadened sufficiently to serve as a
category for a comprehensive theology of Christ,
church, and liturgy. At the same time, when applied to
liturgy, it is elastic enough to take in more than what

scholastic theology referred to as the essence of the sacrament, or its matter and form.

The key notion in symbolic causality is that the symbol is self-expression and coming-to-be through self-expression. Symbol is necessary both to the constitution of a thing's being and to communication. Schillebeeckx's major ontological principle is that for humanity, mutual availability is possible only through bodiliness and that the primary form of bodily communication is symbolic.[15] He explains that communication is based on this principle, not only because the inner mind and heart must be represented in symbol in order to allow for communication, but also because this symbolic representation is necessary to the perfect coming to be of the inner mind and of the human person as such. Thus there is a clear unity between sign and signified, the former not being merely the exteriorization of the latter, but constitutive of its perfect being.[16]

The incarnation is God's self-communication in the mode of human bodiliness, and Christ is thus called the primary sacrament of God's self-giving and revelation. To continue as mediator after the resurrection, Jesus Christ must remain bodily present to the world, and this he does in and through the church. A theology of church as sacrament has its justification in this principle of redemption. The liturgy, or more narrowly the sacrament, being the church's self-expression in grace, is also the sacrament of Christ and the sacrament of God's encounter with humanity in Christ. Both in his early work on sacrament and in his later works, Schillebeeckx gave considerable development to the category of encounter. It is an important key to his notion of what happens in sacrament. While it is of course an encounter in love, more central to Schillebeeckx's thought is an encounter in meaning. Manifesting self to us in Jesus Christ, in the church, and in its liturgy, God proffers to humanity a meaning to life, and on the basis of this shared meaning there is a communion in divine love and a participation in divine reality.

Schillebeeckx invoked this category of meaning to enter the debate over transubstantiation and transsignification[17] and continues to use it in his references to liturgy in works on hermeneutics, Christology, and grace.[18] He thought that transsignification as a category brought out the interpersonal meaning and nature of the eucharistic presence of Christ. He finds that advertence to the meaning of Christ's death as celebrated in the church's worship establishes a link between it and orthopraxis. An obscure point in his theology is the nature of the relation between reality and meaning, and this can be remarked on particularly in his book on the eucharist. There he offers a lengthy phenomenology of meaning and of the way in which it constitutes the human world. Then, however, he goes on to say that transsignification does not say enough about the reality of the eucharistic presence and change, and that consequently it is still necessary to keep the category of substantial change and substantial presence. In his work *Jesus,* he presents the death of Jesus, the ultimate act of his Abba experience, as the consummate revelation of the Word, where the whole meaning of life as gift and grace is manifested. He does not identify the Word or the incarnation with this experience, however, since there remains the ineffable mystery of the trinity of Father, Word, and Spirit, to which it is necessary to refer back as the source and reference point in God's manifestation in Jesus.[19]

Schillebeeckx's refusal to equate reality with meaning is based on his reticence over the extent of the possible objective representation of reality.[20] After all, shared meaning belongs within the order of objective representation. In his understanding of the process of human knowledge, Schillebeeckx believes that a nonconceptual and intuitive grasp of the real occurs simultaneously with conceptual intellection but is not identified with it. This intuition is real knowledge but it defies objective representation. It is present in all representation to make us aware of the limits of this representation in presenting reality, even though such representation can be said to tend toward reality and in that sense to be objective. One can see what happens when this idea is applied to sacrament and to the idea of sacrament as encounter. The divine is really present and really communicated in sacrament, and in this communication God adopts the mode of bodily expression and representative meaning so that a truly personal and human encounter occurs. However, the reality cannot be totally objectified in sacramental representation or totally known as meaning. Hence perfect coincidence between the divine self-communication and that which is represented in sign is not achieved. The sacrament as sign tends towards this reality and allows it to be intuited, but it cannot adequately represent it.

For his part, Karl Rahner posits a closer unity between symbol and symbolized in his notion of the *Realsymbol*.[21] From our knowledge of finite being, it is possible to know that the symbol is constitutive of being and becoming. It is then possible to apply this by way of analogy to God's self-communication, and indeed to the mystery of the Trinity itself. According to Rahner, nothing comes to be except through symbol. The symbol participates in the reality symbolized as the form in which that reality manifests itself and comes to be. The human person does not know and possess the self except through the other of symbolic manifestation, and it is only in this way that the person is truly constituted as such. This is then said to be true of all being, for all being attains its reality in showing itself forth in symbol. This allows for a close unity between the human and the material world, for even simple things like bread and water attain their being when they manifest themselves in symbolic form. To Christ, church, and sacrament, this notion of symbol is applied when they are explained as symbols of divine self-expression and self-communication. This is a communication in which God also comes to be as other, not indeed in the inner mystery of the Trinity but in the reality of the economy of redemption and creation.

In the theory of symbolic causality, whether as proposed by Rahner, or Schillebeeckx, or some other, one no longer talks of God as acting upon the human person through the instrumentality of the sacraments. Instead, one may speak of God present in the symbol, in a process of self-expression and self-communication. Sacramental grace is the human person's communion with God in receiving that gift and in responding to God, likewise through a symbolic self-expression and self-communication, which constitute the person's coming to be.

While there is a strong trend in current Catholic theology to follow up on this notion of symbol, some either see limits to it or look for ways to develop it further. Three points in particular are given more attention than in the original works of Rahner and Schillebeeckx, not only regarding the ontology of symbol's insertion into humanity's coming to be, but also regarding the questions pertinent to God's presence and action. First is the relation of a notion of symbol to a phenomenology of language. Second is the historical dimension of God's self-communication. Third and related closely to this is the relation between the mystery of God and the mystery of divine self-communication. Since this last point belongs more to a theology of God than to the theology of liturgy, we will not treat it here, although its consequences for liturgy are acknowledged.

In his continued writings, Schillebeeckx allows generally in his theology for these perspectives, as well as in a more particular way when he refers to liturgy. The original resurrection experience, which constitutes the reality of revelation, is communicated through the ethical witness of Christians and through the liturgy, before it is explicated in theology. Thus attention to the forms and language of worship is necessary for theological reflection. He has developed his own theological hermeneutics which makes him particularly sensitive to the distortions which can take place in expression and communication. In his book on ministry,[22] he shows how the process of choice and ordination of ministers has been distorted by the intrusion of ideological and nontheological factors. What he says of this has implications for all liturgical development and celebration. Therefore, it follows that demystification of symbol systems is needed to allow freedom to God's communication, and that it means taking account of the historical mode and contingency of this communication. Schillebeeckx makes a link between liturgy and ethics, because on the one hand, liturgy offers the ground for meaningful behavior, and on the other, the conduct of Christians who remain most closely in touch with the original liberating experience of Jesus and the disciples serves as a diagnosis of the distortions which have taken place in church practice, institution, and celebration.

Others would pursue the intrinsicity of language to divine self-communication in other directions. The analysis of limit-situations and of the limit-language which reveals their transcendental openness is pertinent to both a theology of revelation and to a theology of sacrament. Limit-situations are deemed to be the privileged moments of God's self-communication, and a trend in biblical hermeneutics relates particular and typical forms of biblical discourse to these situations. Such situations are those in which persons and communities are particularly sensitive to their finitude on the one hand and to the call beyond it on the other. Some are general, such as birth, death, sexual encounter, severe sickness, and handicap. Others are more particular and specific, such as the tragedies which befall peoples or the limits set on freedom by the incursion of human evil and violence. These have a very strong historical quality. As God's word was spoken to the Jews under the slavery of Pharaoh, so it is listened for in the holocaust of the Jews under the Nazis or in the oppression of tribal and black peoples in Latin America. Some movement is then made to see in sacramental language a limit-language, addressed either to the general human experiences of limit or in a more firmly historical context to the tragedies and oppressions of peoples.[23]

At this point, one takes up the historical dimension of God's self-communication and Schillebeeckx again enters the scene. His critical hermeneutics already has a historical dimension, because it takes note of distortions that take place in the course of history, as well as of the need to address new situations. His very notion of symbolic representation implies attention to the historical, because the limit of objective representation means that it is constantly open to revision. However, historicity is more intrinsic to his notion of revelation and liturgy than these points alone indicate. First, he talks of God as future. By this he means that in virtue of the eschatological nature of revelation, we must see it as bringing us toward God rather than as being in possession of a God already given. Second, in liturgy's expression of divine presence and grace, memory is central. Only in the memory of Jesus and his suffering can all suffering be given expression and meaning, and so become a *locus* of divine communication. When memory of Jesus Christ prevails, instead of institutionalism, and when it brings all suffering to expression, then liturgy itself becomes a critical force developing the tension of meaning which leads humanity toward the future of God.[24]

One way of pursuing the relation of sacrament to history is to adopt the analogy of the work of art in its relation to both creation and history. This analogy has the advantage of holding together both the issue of language and the issue of history.[25] It is said of the work of art that it lets Being stand forth. Things are real in their presence in time and space, but they are partly concealed and must be brought to revealment. It is of the nature of a work of art that it lets things stand forth, lets them become appearances in which their nature and their relatedness to other things is manifest. The creativity of the work of art lets possibilities of forms inherent in things come to be in the human world. The human way of dwelling on earth is to be sensitive to the forms and to the things among which humanity dwells together. Art is a disclosure of being, and the work of art relates more in its being to the things it represents than to the artist. In this sense it is said to be being coming to be through representation, coming from concealment to revealment. Since the aesthetic is nonconceptual and synthetic rather than scientific and analytic, it allows for some coming to explicit meaning through thought, but it also demands reverence before the being which cannot be caught in this type of conceptual discourse and which is intuited in the appreciation of aesthetic form.

When this analogy of the work of art is used of sacrament, sacrament is highlighted as a disclosure of the divine present in the world and of the world constituted in its utmost reality by this presence. It is implied that creation is already a divine self-communication and a symbol in which God in gratuity takes on the form of other. The notion of symbolic causality then recurs as pertinent to creation as well as to the economy of redemption. Revelation is the presence of God in creation and salvation history. It is the manifestation and freeing of that presence in a world of sin. This shows not merely what is already there but is an actual coming to be, a coming from concealment to revealment. In that sense, historical event and its expression in word and sacrament is a creative act, for the manifestation is constitutive of the being, granted the presence of the potential to come to be. To the gratuity of creation is then added the gratuity of redemption. Since sin inhibits and limits humanity's perceptivity and participation in creation, and so inhibits creation's own showing forth of inner forms, the presence of God in Jesus Christ and in the church is redemptive. In Jesus Christ it is revealed that God's presence in the universe is one with suffering. It is a pathos, for the divine love dwells not only in what we naturally think of as creative forces, but it dwells more fully in the limitations put on them by evil and suffering. What is particular to Jesus Christ as sacrament of God's presence is the revelation that suffering too has a form in which this presence shows itself forth. As a memorial of Jesus Christ, the liturgy is analogous to a work of art, for in its own symbolic language and representation it shows forth the presence of the humanity of Jesus in the world as divine pathos. It declares that through the solidarity of Jesus in his abiding presence with all who suffer, the redeeming love of God is at the heart of the world. Liturgy shows forth this presence and redemptive love by calling to mind the past, by attending to the sufferings of the present and giving symbolic expression to the witness of those who live suffering in the freedom of Jesus Christ, and by the imaginative representation of the future, when God's presence comes to full manifestation in the simultaneous liberation of creation and humanity. Since the representation is symbolic and aesthetic, liturgy or sacrament allows for the thought which explicitates meaning, but at another level it demands reverence before the reality which can only be symbolized and not brought to full conceptualization.

Since this analogy of the work of art posits a divine force and presence at the heart of creation, it can be pursued further by adopting some of the positions of a Spirit christology.[26] The Spirit of God is present in creation from the beginning, and the act of creation is itself a divine self-communication. The full meaning and coming to be of this Spirit in the world is given only in the incarnation of the Logos, when in Jesus Christ, God's loving, creative, and redemptive presence is made manifest and comes to be in a new way. This self-disclosure of God in Jesus Christ reaches its consummation in the resurrection, and with it there is a creative release of the power of the Spirit in the world, so that the metaphor of a new creation is truly revealing. The memory of this event (which can be understood either through the metaphor of *Pascha/Passio* or through that of *Pascha/Transitus*, with the inevitable consequences for meaning) kept by the church in liturgy shows forth in symbolic form the presence of the Spirit in the world and in history.

In brief outline, these are some of the ways in which Catholic sacramental and liturgical theology includes an ontology. The lines here presented seem most pertinent to the renewal of symbolic liturgy and symbolic universe postulated in the first chapter. First, the notion of symbolic causality was presented as an alternative to efficient causality. Then it was related to the interpretation of language as the particular sacramental means of divine self-communication. Third, it was pointed out that this communication occurs within history and is expressed as historical in liturgy. Fourth, the analogy of the work of art was mentioned as a way of satisfying the relation between historical actualization and creative divine presence, and as a way of developing further the idea of symbolic causality. Fifth, the affinities between this and a Spirit christology were suggested. All of this has the advantage of not appealing to a hierarchical vision of church and universe or to a hierarchy of sacramental causes. Instead, it appeals to a creative and redeeming presence in the world, which shows itself in history through event and symbolization. This symbolization is intrinsic to the mystery of the incarnation and of the church. It is simultaneously a work of God and of the church which celebrates in memory and hope. Here is an ontology which makes room for a developing liturgy, since in keeping memory in the power of the Spirit, the church encompasses into Christ's mystery new realities and new events. It speaks his name in new ways and in new forms, which are ever traditional and ever new. Not only in its work of witness but in tandem with this in its liturgy, the church participates in the redeeming and creative presence of God in history, since through its liturgy this presence is shown forth, and in being shown forth this presence comes to be.

THE WORLD OF SACRAMENTAL REPRESENTATION
From this ontology of symbol's insertion into the human and of its nature as God's self-communication, it is possible to think of the world into which liturgy invites its participants. Paul Ricoeur points out that in its ordering and expressing of the world in which people live, every symbol system has to do with power, with having, and with value.[27] These three things can provide the lines for suggesting some items for reflection on the world of sacramental representation,

and on its contrast with the historical tendencies of the Western culture.

In the society that we daily observe, power is with the strong. Those who have more get more. Value is measured by what one can achieve and possess and by the extent of the power that one can wield. The nuclear arms race is but a large-scale projection of all that we are fast becoming. It is our ideology, a world held in balance by domination, superior force, and fear of extinction.

Liturgy calls us to recognize our boundedness, to desire salvation by grace and not by works. "Where sin abounded, grace does more abound" is its leitmotiv. Boundedness has to do with nature and the cosmos, whose exploitation redounds to our own detriment and whose awesomeness is given in bread and wine. It has to do with the person's boundedness to community and society, which is celebrated in a common table. It has to do with language, whose possibilities are exhausted only because we have tried to *use* it and have stopped *listening* to it, and whose power is contained in the single word "Abba." It has to do with the boundedness of the psyché, whose depths we must recognize but in whose exploration we must at some point cease, standing still before the need to be forgiven by another, to receive healing and wholeness which is not in our power.

In the world of liturgy, things and words are not instrumentalized but celebrated and contemplated. Things and actions are not used as instruments to produce something, but the revelation they bear is received only in contemplation, in a reverence for how they draw together "earth, sky, gods and mortals." Words are not functional and scientific but poetic. Language is always at its breaking point, and on this condition being is revealed in it. Language recognizes its limits and seeks new interplay of meanings and images in the hope of new perspective and wonder. It is humble, for it acknowledges the nonidentity between being and language, above all between God and any name that is spoken of the divine.

Power

All that the liturgy represents about power, having, and value can be summed up in the one word "gift," or "freely given." The words used for "power" in the gospels are associated with Jesus' being the one sent by God, the one sent because, taking on all the tenderness and compassion of mother and father, husband and wife, God first loved us. They are words like *exousia*, which is not a domination but a gospel, a word which is spoken and which liberates. It is a word to be received and hearkened to and which, when taken as gift, empowers. It is a word which heals and reconciles when received in faith as God's own gift. Power proclaimed as *diakonia* announces that God came among us in the form of a servant, that Jesus saved because he served, that in serving he empowered. The saving power of God is as much present today in the one who serves at table as in the one who presides. *Dynamis* speaks of Christ and Christians as people possessed by the Spirit, people in whom the energy of God's Spirit is at work because God's love overflows in their hearts. It is an energy which shows itself only in gifts of service, not in control and domination. Of the source, origin, and nature of power, liturgy speaks in memory of Jesus Christ and his self-emptying, and in the invocation of the Holy Spirit. This power dwells in the act of praise spoken by the community, in the sharing of a common table, and in deeds of healing. The church has no power except in the memory of Jesus Christ, in the remembrance of his suffering and death, of his solidarity with all victims, and of the great power of compassion, of which his death was the climax and witness. To receive the power of that memory, to give freedom to the Spirit that is given, the liturgy constantly retells the story and sings the hymns which celebrate how God's mercy takes our very boundedness as the place of the revelation of power and love. This is the power of one who said "blessed are the poor," "blessed are the persecuted," "blessed are those who hunger and thirst after justice." One cannot remember Jesus, nor share in the power of God, without remembering those who have become victims of domination and those who in a greater hope protest by their lives this unholy distribution of power. In liturgy, the church remembers all who are dominated, all of nature's loveliness that is suppressed, all who resist, and all who testify. It is thus that it touches God's presence and power in the world.

Having
The gospel's and the liturgy's symbol of "having" is poverty. It is the economy of means, the simplicity of a table, the purity of the water that flows, the touch of hands that possess nothing other than their touch, that have no other instruments. Poverty is first the sense of possessing nothing, yet having all. It belongs only to those who know the meaning of gift. It is then the sense of value exhibited in the economy of means, in the simplicity of those gestures which signify the common life. Poverty is this common life, where domination and riches and social status and hierarchical distinction count for nothing, where there is no precedence or privilege, except that granted to the poor, whether by reason of social force or by reason of choice. Poverty is the word, the song of lamentation and praise, the magnificat of those whom God lifts up. Poverty is the one remembered, the one who dies that we might become rich. These are the only things that the church has and that it calls its own, and these it has because it has received them.

Value

The liturgy's word for "value" is the overflow of grace. In celebrating the initiative of God's love and the excellence of God's mercy, it expresses the roots of value and esteem. From this comes the Christian's self-esteem. From this self-esteem comes the esteem that Christians have for others and for the supreme value, which is communion with God. The church can celebrate itself as the holy people, the race set apart, the royal priesthood, the living temple, because God has first loved us, and nothing can separate us from the love of God which is in Christ Jesus. In this esteem, Christian people stand firm against all that disvalues in this world. They can celebrate the world as God's kingdom, because liberation is a promise given to it. This is a hope which makes of liturgy the imagination of the impossible, of the new heaven and the new earth, where there is no need for sun nor moon because the Lamb will be the light.

NOTES

1. On the place of the visual in worship, see Nathan Mitchell, *Cult and Controversy. The Worship of the Eucharist Outside Mass* (New York: Pueblo, 1982), pp. 375–89.

2. Ibid., pp. 163–83.

3. Maurice Wiles, "Origen as biblical scholar," *Cambridge History of the Bible,* vol. 1 (Cambridge: Cambridge University Press, 1970), pp. 454–88.

4. See chapter 2.

5. This explanation was embraced by Pius XII, *Mediator Dei,* AAS 39 (1947), p. 548.

6. Paul Ricoeur, " 'Original sin': A study in meaning," in *The Conflict of Interpretations* (Evanston, Ill.: Northwestern, 1974), pp. 269–86.

7. On contrast experiences as diagnostic of ministerial situations, see Edward Schillebeeckx, *Ministry: Leadership in*

the Community of Jesus Christ (New York: Crossroad, 1981), pp. 75–85.

8. Victor W. Turner, *The Ritual Process: Structure and Anti-Structure* (London: Routledge & Kegan Paul, 1969), pp. 94–165.

9. Victor W. Turner, "Ritual, tribal and catholic," *Worship* 50 (1976), 504–26.

10. David Power, "The song of the lord in an alien land," *Concilium* 92 (New York: Herder & Herder, 1974), pp. 85–106.

11. Anscar Vonier, *A Key to the Doctrine of the Eucharist* (London: Burns Oates & Washbourne, 1925).

12. G. H. Williams, "The sacramental presupposition of Anselm's Cur Deus Homo," *Church History* 26 (1957), pp. 245–74.

13. Ray Hart, *Unfinished Man and the Imagination* (New York: Herder & Herder, 1968).

14. Karl Rahner, "The theology of the symbol," *Theological Investigations* IV (New York: Seabury Press, 1964), pp. 221–52; Edward Schillebeeckx, *Christ the Sacrament of the Encounter with God,* translated by Cornelius Ernst. (Kansas City: Sheed Andrews & McMeel, 1963).

15. Schillebeeckx, *Christ the Sacrament,* pp. 3–10.

16. Ibid., pp. 63–65.

17. Edward Schillebeeckx, *The Eucharist* (New York: Sheed & Ward, 1968).

18. Edward Schillebeeckx, *Understanding the Faith* (New York: Seabury Press, 1974), pp. 17–19, 63, 68; and *Christ: the Experience of Jesus as Lord* (New York: Seabury Press, 1980), pp. 98–101, 146–47, 811–18.

19. Edward Schillebeeckx, *Jesus: An Experiment in Christology* (New York: Seabury Press, 1979), pp. 636–68.

20. Edward Schillebeeckx, *Revelation and Theology,* vol. 2 (New York: Sheed & Ward, 1968), pp. 18, 165, 181–93.

211

21. Rahner, "The theology of the symbol."

22. Schillebeeckx, *Ministry*, pp. 56–58.

23. Leonardo Boff, *Os Sacramentos da Vida e a Vida dos Sacramentos: Enscio de Teologia Narrativa* (Petrópolis, Brazil: Vozes 1975); Mark Searle, "The pedagogical function of the liturgy," *Worship* 55 (1981), 332–59; Tissa Balasuriya, *The Eucharist and Human Liberation* (Maryknoll, N.Y.: Orbis, 1979); Rafael Avila, *Worship and Politics* (Maryknoll, N.Y.: Orbis, 1981).

24. Schillebeeckx, *Christ: the Experience of Jesus as Lord*, pp. 811–18.

25. See the discussion in chapter 1 on Winter's *Liberating Creation*.

26. Walter Kasper, *Jesus the Christ* (New York: Paulist Press, 1976); Philip J. Rosato, "Spirit christology: Ambiguity and promise," *Theological Studies* 38 (1977), 423–49.

27. Paul Ricoeur, "The Tasks of the Political Educator," *Philosophy Today* 17 (1973), 142–52.

Conclusion: The Truth of Sacrament

When sacraments were viewed primarily as means of
grace, the effect of their administration could be
guaranteed by the simple dictum that when sacraments
are validly celebrated and no obstacle occurs on the
part of the subject, grace is conferred. When, however,
due to a retrieval of both collective and individual
subject, sacraments are considered in terms of
consciousness, intentionality, and appropriation of a
world, their truth becomes the issue of their meaning
and of their fidelity to the gospel tradition. They cannot
themselves guarantee their own truth, or right conduct
and grace. Like any other expression of the faith, for
example dogma, they must be submitted to certain
criteria, on the basis of which their fidelity and truth
may be assessed.

It seems appropriate to suggest, based on what has
been said in previous chapters, that there are three
criteria for validating sacramental practice. These are
the fullness of language, adequacy to experience, and
celebration's relation to the orthopraxis of gospel
freedom and solidarity with the suffering.

The criterion of fullness of language is both historical
and anthropological. It derives from what has been said
about the sacramental canon and about liturgy's
integration of the language of ritual, myth, and
metaphor. For example, since the sacramental canon
gives central importance in celebration to a prayer of
thanksgiving and intercession, one must still remain

213

dubious about the formula for reconciliation in the new Rite of Penance, since it is a compromise between laudatory, intercessory, and declaratory forms.[1] Similarly, on the basis of an anthropology of language, the English translation of the third eucharistic prayer in the Roman Sacramentary must be criticized for its failure to appreciate the metaphorical nature of sacrificial language, or in other words, because it seems to reduce its usage to univocal expression.[2] These are not merely stylistic niceties but raise genuine concerns about the truth of celebration, or the way it carries its participants forward in the quest for truth.

In a way, the criterion of adequacy to experience has been the theme of this entire work. The question of the model put to use in liturgy and of its relation to culture was raised in the first chapter. It was there remarked that a hierarchical model is not adequate to contemporary experience. Humanity's current possibilities and needs cannot be transferred meaningfully into such a model. Hence, a critical issue for liturgy is the appropriation of traditional symbols within a historical and anthropological model.

The issues of our age, whether they be those of industrial exploitation or deprivation of rights or nuclear warfare or global relations, are political issues because they concern the distribution and use of power. The lack of a historical sense in a Christian community's participation in these issues is fatal, as is any naiveté about good and evil. What is needed in liturgy is an expression of hope in an age which is heavily politicized and deeply conscious of the historical. Liturgical symbolism and prayer have always spoken to the presence of evil in the world, but these evils have all too often been identified with the enemies of the establishment. It must be admitted that today the reverse bias is sometimes found: only the revolutionary is claimed as the good Christian and economic capitalism may be as wrathfully denounced as were the medieval devils which infested the cooking pots and the cornfields. In fact, the human condition is much more ambiguous. Symbols of evil and power alike can reveal the blindness and enigma of the human enterprise, and warn us that there is no easy discernment of the forces of evil nor any easy retrieval of the forces of good. The issue is whether people may live in hope in the midst of uncertainty and struggle. This is possible if, through images of hope, the church can today project the power that comes through the remembrance of Jesus Christ.

The Jewish people came to know Yahweh through the interpretation of historical and political events. In virtue of this, they came into being as a single people and nation. Events prior to, and subsequent to, the Exodus were interpreted in the light of this paradigmatic event. Critical exegesis has made us increasingly aware of the difficulties and controversies surrounding such interpretation, so we should not think of it as an easy thing to do, or as always crystal clear. A good example is history's view of the Davidic story. Different interpretations of that story are found in the Bible, different ways in which the same episodes are narrated according to how the tradition viewed the central figure and his dynasty. The important thing was to recover the hope inherent in the original event and to see its repercussions on the ethical, the social, and the political.

If the historical and anthropological is taken as the model for liturgical renewal and development, the community can find in sacrament a vision which allows it to approach its own participation in the affairs of the time and to live in hope, even if often in puzzlement. The eschatological perception of events and of history which the celebration of the death and resurrection of Christ fosters makes it possible to look forward in hope, while at the same time realizing the provisional nature of political choice and action. By the same token, it allows some pluriformity in that choice because it reckons with the ambiguity of human action and with the darkness or blindness of evil.

This relation of symbol to historical and political experience leads to the last criterion of sacramental truth, which is the experience of the cross and solidarity with those who suffer. This norm says that liturgy is never its own justification. It does not establish its own truth. Such truth depends on the conjunction between liturgy and ethics, in other words, on the conjunction between liturgy and that particular religious experience which is central to Christianity, the experience of the cross. Since taking up one's cross identifies one with Jesus Christ, the experience is that of solidarity with the suffering of the world. Within that solidarity is the experience of hope. The believer knows that in the darkness one is not abandoned by God, and it is possible to expect the kingdom divinely promised. This experience is concrete, not abstract. It is the experience of those who in the name of Jesus Christ live lives inspired by the Beatitudes. In a period of liturgical crisis, it is important for the whole church to look to the contrast experiences and the contrast liturgical models provided by those communities that live the struggle for freedom in faith and hope.[3] The orthodoxy of the sacramental canon is verified or authenticated by the orthopraxis of solidarity with victims and of hope in suffering.

NOTES

1. *The Rites of the Catholic Church*, vol. 1 (New York: Pueblo, 1976), pp. 372–73.

2. When the Latin *hostia* is rendered as *victim*, polysemy has given way to univocity.

3. Some of the issues are explored in *Concilium* 152, *Can We Always Celebrate the Eucharist?*, Mary Collins & David Power (eds.) (New York: Seabury, 1982).

Selected Bibliography

Aubry, André. "The feast of peoples and the explosion of society—Popular practice and liturgical practice." In David Power (ed.), *Times of Celebration, Concilium* 142, New York: Seabury Press, 1981, pp. 55–64.

Auerbach, Eric. *Mimesis.* Princeton, N.J.: Princeton University Press, 1953.

Avila, Rafael. *Worship and Politics.* Maryknoll, N.Y.: Orbis, 1981.

Balthasar, Hans Urs Von. *Love Alone: The Way of Revelation.* New York: Herder & Herder, 1969.

Baptism, Eucharist and Ministry. Faith & Order Paper No. 111. Geneva: World Council of Churches, 1982.

Bastide, Roger. *The African Religions of Brazil. Towards a Sociology of the Interpenetration of Civilizations.* Baltimore: Johns Hopkins University Press, 1978.

Berger, Blandine-Dominique. *Le Drame Liturgique de Pâques: Liturgie et Théatre.* Paris: Beauchesne, 1976.

Biemer, Günter. "Controversy on the age of confirmation as a typical example of conflict between the criteria of theology and the demands of pastoral practice." In Luis Maldonado & David Power (eds.), *Liturgy and Human Passage, Concilium* 112. New York: Seabury Press, 1979.

Boff, Leonardo. *Os Sacramentos da Vida e a Vida dos Sacramentos. Enscio de Teologia Narrativa.* Petrópolis, Brazil: Vozes, 1975.

Bouyer, Louis. *Eucharist: Theology and Spirituality of the*

217

Eucharistic Prayer. Notre Dame, Ind.: University of Notre Dame Press, 1968.

———. *Le Père Invisible.* Paris: Cerf, 1976.

———. *Rite and Man: Natural Sacredness and Christian Liturgy.* London: Burns & Oates, 1963.

Brinkman, B. R. "On sacramental man." *Heythrop Journal* 13 (1972), 371–401; 14 (1973), 5–39, 162–89, 280–306, 396–416.

Brown, Terence. *Ireland: A Social and Cultural History 1922–79.* Glasgow: Fontana Paperbacks, 1981.

Brueggemann, Walter. *The Prophetic Imagination.* Philadelphia: Fortress Press, 1980.

Burkhardt, John E. *Worship.* Philadelphia: Westminster Press, 1982.

Campbell, Joseph. *The Masks of God,* vol. 4 of *Creative Mythology.* New York: Viking Press, 1968.

Casel, Odo. *The Mystery of Christian Worship.* Westminster, Md.: Newman Press, 1962.

Chauvet, Louis-Marie. *Du Symbolique au Symbole: Essai sur les Sacrements.* Paris: Cerf, 1979.

———. "La ritualité dans le cercle infernal du symbole." *La Maison-Dieu* 133:1 (1978), 31–77.

Chenu, Marie-Dominique. *Nature, Man and Society in the Twelfth Century,* selected, edited, and translated by Jerome Taylor & Lester K. Little. Chicago: University of Chicago Press, 1979.

Chevalier, Jean-Alain Gheerbrant. *Dictionnaire des Symboles. Mythes, Rêves, Coutumes, Gestes, Formes, Figures, Couleurs, Nombres.* 4 vols. Paris: Seghers & Jupiter, 1973/74.

Childs, Brevard. *Memory and Tradition in Israel.* Naperville, Tenn.: Allenson, 1962.

Chupungco, Anscar J. *The Cosmic Elements of Christian Passover.* Rome: San Anselmo, 1977.

———. "Liturgical feasts and the seasons of the year." In David Power (ed.), *Times of Celebration, Concilium* 142. New York: Seabury, 1981, pp. 31–36.

————. *Cultural Adaptation of the Liturgy*. New York: Paulist Press, 1982.

Collins, Mary & David Power (eds.). *Can We Always Celebrate the Eucharist? Concilium* 152. New York: Seabury, 1982.

Corriveau, R. *The Liturgy of Life. A Study of the Ethical Thought of St. Paul in His Letters to the Early Christian Communities.* Brussels-Montreal: Bellarmin, 1970.

Couch, Beatriz Melano. "Religious symbols and philosophical reflection." In Charles E. Reagan (ed.), *Studies in the Philosophy of Paul Ricoeur*, pp. 115–131. Athens: Ohio University Press, 1979.

Cox, Harvey. *Feast of Fools*. Cambridge, Mass.: Harvard University Press, 1969.

Crites, Stephen. "The narrative quality of experience." *Journal of the Academy of Religion* 39 (1971), 291–311.

Crossan, Dominic. *In Parables*. New York: Harper & Row, 1973.

————. *The Dark Interval. Towards a Theology of Story*. Niles, Ill.: Argus, 1975.

Daly, Robert J. *Christian Sacrifice. The Judaeo-Christian Background before Origen*. Washington, D.C.: Catholic University of America Press, 1978.

Doran, Robert. "Psychic conversion." *The Thomist* 41 (1977), 200–36.

————. "Aesthetic subjectivity and generalized empirical method." *The Thomist* 43 (1979), 257–78.

Douglas, Mary. *Purity and Danger. An Analysis of Concepts of Pollution and Taboo*. London: Routledge & Kegan Paul, 1966.

————. *Natural Symbols. Explorations in Cosmology*. New York: Pantheon, 1970.

Dunne, John S. *A Search for God in Time and Memory*. Notre Dame, Ind.: University of Notre Dame Press, 1977.

Dupont, Jacques. "Ceci est mon corps, ceci est mon sang." *Nouvelle Revue Théologique* 80 (1958), 1025–41.

Duquoc, Christian. *Dieu Différent.* Paris: Cerf, 1977.

Durand, Gilbert. *L'Imagination Symbolique.* Paris: Presses Universitaires, 1968.

————. *Les Structures Anthropologiques de l'Imaginaire. Introduction à l'Archétypologie Général.* Paris: Bordas, 1969.

Eliade, Mircea. *Images and Symbols.* London: Harvill, 1961.

————. *The Sacred and the Profane. The Nature of Religion.* New York: Harcourt Brace & World, 1959.

Frye, Northrop. *Anatomy of Criticism.* Princeton: Princeton University Press, 1957.

————. "New directions from old." In Henry A. Murray (ed.), *Myth and Mythmaking,* pp. 115–31. Boston: Beacon Press, 1961.

————. *The Great Code. The Bible and Literature.* New York: Harcourt Brace Jovanovich, 1982.

Gadamer, Hans-Georg. *Truth and Method.* New York: Crossroad, 1982.

————. *Philosophical Hermeneutics.* Berkeley: University of California Press, 1977.

————. "Religious and poetical speaking." In Alan M. Olson (ed.), *Myth, Symbol, and Reality.* Notre Dame, Ind.: University of Notre Dame Press, 1980, pp. 86–98.

Gaiffre, B. de. "La lecture des Actes des Martyrs dans la prière liturgique en occident." *Analecta Bollandiana* 72 (1954), 134–66.

Gavin, F. *The Jewish Antecedents of the Christian Eucharist.* New York: Ktav, 1969.

Geertz, Clifford. *The Interpretation of Cultures.* New York: Basic Books, 1973.

Geffré, Claude. "Father as the proper name of God." In Johann B. Metz & Edward Schillebeeckx, *God as Father?, Concilium* 143, 43–50. New York: Seabury, 1981, 43–50.

Gilkey, Langdon. *Society and the Sacred.* New York: Crossroad, 1981.

Gryson, Roger. *Les Origines du Célibat Ecclésiastique du premier au septième siècle.* Gembloux: Duculot, 1970.

Guthrie, Harvey H. *Theology as Thanksgiving. From Israel's Psalms to the Church's Eucharist.* New York: Seabury, 1981.

Guzie, Tad. *The Book of Sacramental Basics.* New York: Paulist Press, 1981.

Hahn, Ferdinand. *The Worship of the Early Church.* Translated by David E. Green with an introduction by John Reumann. Philadelphia: Fortress, 1973.

Hamerton-Kelly, Robert. *God the Father: Theology and Patriarchy in the Teaching of Jesus.* Philadelphia: Fortress, 1979.

Hamman, Adalbert. "La résurrection du Christ dans l'antiquité Chrétienne." *Revue des Sciences Religieuses* 50 (1976), 1–24.

Happel, Stephen. "The structure of our utopian mitsein (life-together)." In Schillebeeckx, Edward & Bas Van Iersel (eds.), *Heaven, Concilium* 123. New York: Seabury, 1979.

————. "The 'bent world': Sacrament as orthopraxis." *CTSA Proceedings* 35 (1980), 88–101.

————. "Prayer and sacrament. A role in foundational theology." *The Thomist* 45 (1981), 243–61.

Hardison, O. B. *Christian Rite and Christian Drama in the Middle Ages.* Baltimore: Johns Hopkins University Press, 1965.

Häring, N. M. "Berengar's definitions of sacramentum and their influence on medieval sacramentology." *Medieval Studies* 10 (1948), 109–46.

————. "St. Augustine's use of the word character." *Medieval Studies* 14 (1952), 79–97.

Hart, Ray. *Unfinished Man and the Imagination.* New York: Herder & Herder, 1968.

Heidegger, Martin. *Poetry, Language, Thought.* New York: Harper & Row, 1975.

Holeton, D. "The sacramental language of St. Leo the Great.

A study of the words 'munus' and 'oblata.' " *Ephemerides Liturgicae* 92 (1978), 115–65.

Huizinga, Johan. *Homo Ludens. A Study of the Play-Element in Culture.* Boston: Beacon Press, 1955.

Jeremias, Joachim. *The Eucharistic Words of Jesus.* Philadelphia: Fortress, 1977.

Jossua, Jean-Pierre. "La Constitution 'Sacrosanctum Concilium' dans l'ensemble de l'oeuvre conciliaire." In J.-P. Jossua & Y. Congar (eds.), *La Liturgie après Vatican II* Paris: Cerf, 1967.

Joyce, James. *A Portrait of the Artist as a Young Man.* New York: Penguin Books, 1964.

Jungmann, Josef. *The Place of Christ in Liturgical Prayer.* New York: Alba, 1965.

Kasper, Walter. *Jesus the Christ.* New York: Paulist Press, 1976.

Kilmartin, Edward J. "When is marriage a sacrament?" *Theological Studies* 34 (1973), 275–86.

————. "Sacrificium laudis. Content and function of early eucharistic prayers." *Theological Studies* 35 (1974), 268–87.

Kretschmar, Georg. "Christliches Pascha im 2. Jahrhundert und die Ausbildung der christlichen Theologie." *Recherches de Sciences Religieuses* 60 (1972), 287–323.

Lamb, Matthew. *Solidarity with Victims. Towards a Theology of Social Transformation.* New York: Crossroad, 1982.

Langer, Susanne K. *Feeling and Form. A Theory of Art.* New York: Scribner's, 1953.

————. *Philosophy in a New Key. A Study in the Symbolism of Reason, Rite, and Art.* Cambridge, Mass.: Harvard University Press, 1978.

————. *Problems of Art. Ten Philosophical Lectures.* New York: Scribner's, 1957.

Léon-Dufour, Xavier. "Das letzte Mahl Jesu und die

testamentarische Tradition nach Lk. 22." *Zeitschrift für katholische Theologie* 103 (1981), 33–55.

Ligier, Louis. "The origins of the eucharistic prayer." *Studia Liturgica* 9 (1973), 161–85.

Little, Lester K. *Religious Poverty and the Profit Economy in Medieval Europe.* Ithaca, N.Y.: Cornell University Press, 1978.

Lonergan, Bernard. *Method in Theology.* New York: Herder & Herder, 1972.

Lourdes 1971: L'Eglise Signe de Salut au Milieu des Hommes. Rapport de l'Assemblée Episcopale de France. Paris: Centurion, 1972.

Lynch, William F. *Christ and Apollo. The Dimensions of the Literary Imagination.* New York: New American Library, 1963.

Maldonado, Luis & David Power (eds.). *Liturgy and Human Passage, Concilium* 112. New York: Seabury, 1979.

McFague, Sallie. *Speaking in Parables. A Study in Metaphor and Theology.* Philadelphia: Fortress, 1975.

Metz, Johann B. *Faith in History and Society. Toward a Practical Fundamental Theology.* New York: Seabury Press, 1980.

Metz, Johann B. & Edward Schillebeeckx (eds.). *God as Father?, Concilium* 143. New York: Seabury, 1981.

Mitchell, Nathan. *Cult and Controversy. The Worship of the Eucharist Outside Mass.* New York: Pueblo, 1982.

Mollat, Michel. "The poverty of Francis: A Christian and social option." In Christian Duquoc & Casiano Floristán, (eds.), *Francis of Assisi Today, Concilium* 149. New York: Seabury, 1981, pp. 23–29.

Alan M. Olson (ed.). *Myth, Symbol, and Reality.* Notre Dame, Ind.: University of Notre Dame Press, 1980.

Neusner, Jacob. "Map without territory: Mishnah's system of sacrifice and sanctuary." *History of Religions* 19 (1979), 103–27.

Oesterley, W. O. E. *The Jewish Background of the Christian Liturgy.* New York: Oxford University Press, 1925.

Otto, Eckart & Tim Schramm. *Festival and Joy.* Nashville: Abingdon, 1980.

Otto, Rudolf. *The Idea of the Holy. An Inquiry into the Non-Rational in an Idea of the Divine and its Relation to the Rational.* Translated from the 9th German ed. by J. Harvey. London: Penguin, 1959.

Perrin, Norman. "The interpretation of a biblical symbol." *Journal of Religion* 55 (1975), 348–70.

Perrot, Charles. "L'Eucharistie dans le Nouveau Testament." *La Maison-Dieu* 167:1 (1979), 109–25.

Pohier, Jacques. *Au Nom du Père. Recherches Théologiques et Psychanalytiques.* Paris: Cerf, 1972.

Pokorný, P. "Christologie et baptême à l'epoque du Christianisme primitif." *New Testament Studies* 27 (1981), 368–80.

Power, David. "The song of the lord in an alien land." In Herman Schmidt & David Power (eds.), *Politics and Liturgy, Concilium* 92. New York: Herder & Herder, 1974.

———. "The odyssey of man in Christ." In Luis Maldonado & David Power (eds.), *Liturgy and Human Passage, Concilium* 112. New York: Seabury Press, 1979.

——— (ed.). *Times of Celebration, Concilium* 142. New York: Seabury Press, 1981.

Rahner, Karl. "The theology of the symbol." In *Theological Investigations* IV. New York: Seabury, 1964, pp. 221–52.

Ricoeur, Paul. *The Conflict of Interpretations: Essays in Hermeneutics,* translated by Don Ihde. Evanston, Ill.: Northwestern University Press, 1974.

———. "Creativity in language." *Philosophy Today* 17 (1973), 97–111.

———. *Freud and Philosophy. An Essay on Interpretation,* translated by D. Savage. New Haven: Yale University Press, 1970.

224

————. *Interpretation Theory: Discourse and the Surplus of Meaning.* Fort Worth: Texas Christian University Press, 1976.

————. "Manifestation et proclamation." *Archivio di Filosofia* 44 (1974), 57–76.

————. "Metaphor and the main problem of hermeneutics." *New Literary History* 6 (1974/75), 95–110.

————. "The narrative function." *Semeia* 13 (1978), 177–202.

————. "Narrative time." *Critical Inquiry* 7 (1980), 169–90.

————. *The Role of Metaphor.* Translated by Robert Czerny with Kathleen McLaughlin & John Costello. Toronto: University of Toronto Press, 1977.

————. *The Symbolism of Evil.* Translated by Emerson Buchanan. Boston: Beacon Press, 1967.

————. "The tasks of the political educator today." *Philosophy Today* 17 (1973), 142–52.

————. *The Philosophy of Paul Ricoeur: An Anthology of His Work.* Edited by Charles E. Reagan & David Stewart. Boston: Beacon Press, 1978.

————. *Essays on Biblical Interpretation.* Edited with an introduction by Lewis S. Mudge. Philadelphia: Fortress, 1980.

Riley, Hugh. M. *Christian Initiation: A Comparative Study of the Interpretation of the Baptismal Liturgy in the Mystagogical Writings of Cyril of Jerusalem, John Chrysostom, Theodore of Mopsuestia and Ambrose of Milan.* Washington, D.C.: Catholic University of America Press, 1974.

Rosato, Philip J. "Spirit christology: ambiguity and promise." *Theological Studies* 38 (1977), 623–49.

Schaldenbrand, Mary. "Metaphoric imagination: Kinship through conflict." In Charles E. Reagan (ed.), *Studies in the Philosophy of Paul Ricoeur,* Athens: Ohio University Press, 1979, pp. 57–81.

Scheer, Anthonius. "Is the Easter Vigil a rite of passage?" In Luis Maldonado & David Power (eds.), *Liturgy and Human Passage, Concilium* 112. New York: Seabury Press, 1979, pp. 50–62.

Schillebeeckx, Edward. *Christ: The Experience of Jesus as Lord.* Translated by John Bowden. New York: Seabury Press, 1980.

―――. *Christ the Sacrament of the Encounter with God.* Translated by Cornelius Ernst. Kansas City: Sheed Andrews & McMeel, 1963.

―――. *The Eucharist.* Translated by N. D. Smith. New York: Sheed & Ward, 1968.

―――. *Jesus: An Experiment in Christology.* Translated by Hubert Hoskins. New York: Seabury Press, 1979.

―――. *Ministry: Leadership in the Community of Jesus Christ.* New York: Crossroad, 1981.

―――. *Revelation and Theology,* vol. 2. Translated by N. D. Smith. New York: Sheed & Ward, 1968.

―――. *Understanding the Faith. Interpretation and Criticism.* Translated by N. D. Smith. New York: Seabury Press, 1974.

Scholes, Robert & Robert Kellogg. *The Nature of Narrative.* New York: Oxford University Press, 1966.

Searle, Mark. "The pedagogical function of the liturgy." *Worship* 55 (1981), 332–59.

Segundo, Juan Luis. *Sacraments Today.* Maryknoll, N.Y.: Orbis, 1973.

Smith, Jonathan Z. "The bare facts of ritual." *History of Religions* 20 (1980), 112–27.

―――. *Map is Not Territory. Studies in the History of Religions.* Leiden: Brill, 1978.

Spinks, Brian. "The anaphora for India: Some theological objections to an attempt of inculturation." *Ephemerides Liturgicae* 95 (1981), 529–49.

Torrance, Thomas. *Theology in Reconciliation.* London: Chapman, 1975.

Tracy, David. *Blessed Rage for Order: The New Pluralism in Theology.* New York: Seabury Press, 1975.

Turner, Victor W. *The Ritual Process: Structure and Anti-Structure.* London: Routledge & Kegan Paul, 1969.

226

———. "Ritual, tribal and catholic." *Worship* 50 (1976), 504–26.

Vergote, Antoine. "The chiasm of subjective and objective functions in the symbol." *Kerygma* 14 (1980), 27–49.

———. *Interprétation du Langage Religieux.* Paris: Seuil, 1974.

Vonier, Anscar. *A Key to the Doctrine of the Eucharist.* London: Burns Oates & Washbourne, 1925.

Weber, Hans-Ruedi. *The Cross: Tradition and Interpretation.* Translated by Elke Jessett. Grand Rapids, Mich.: Eerdmans, 1979.

Weinrich, H. "Narrative theology." In J. B. Metz & J.-P. Jossua, *The Crisis of Religious Language, Concilium* 85. New York: Herder & Herder, 1973.

Westermann, Claus. *Praise and Lament in the Psalms.* Translated by Keith R. Crim & Richard N. Soulen. Atlanta: John Knox Press, 1981.

Wheelwright, Philip. *Metaphor and Reality.* Bloomington: Indiana University Press, 1962.

Williams, G. H. "The sacramental presuppositions of Anselm's Cur Deus Homo." *Church History* 26 (1957), 245–74.

Winter, Gibson. *Liberating Creation: Foundations of Religious Social Ethics.* New York: Crossroad, 1981.

Worgul, George S. *From Magic to Metaphor: A Validation of the Christian Sacraments.* New York: Paulist Press, 1980.

Yarnold, Edward. *The Awe Inspiring Rites of Initiation: Baptismal Homilies of the Fourth Century.* Slough: St. Paul Publications, 1971.

Young, Frances M. *Sacrifice and the Death of Christ.* Philadelphia: Fortress, 1975.

Zenger, Erich. "Ritual and criticism of ritual in the Old Testament." In Luis Maldonado & David Power (eds.), *Liturgy and Human Passage, Concilium* 112. New York: Seabury, 1979.

Index

Change, 7, 10, 12f., 19, 55, 75, 79, 85, 86

Christ, 25, 36, 37, 42, 43, 45, 46, 47, 49, 52, 53, 54–56, 65f., 70, 78, 93, 95, 97, 98, 102, 103, 117, 118, 137, 145, 147, 196, 197, 198. *See also* Jesus, Jesus Christ

Clergy, 16, 46, 51, 52, 53

Commemoration, 35, 38, 62, 94, 108

Communitas, 179f.

Community, 3, 5, 12, 14, 17, 20, 27f., 35–38, 40, 42, 66f., 70, 72, 87, 91f., 95f., 97, 98, 100, 128, 129, 146f.

Contemplation, 50, 51, 68, 78, 79, 121

Cosmic, 39, 42, 47, 76, 89, 91, 93–99, 103, 105, 131, 136, 167, 172

Cosmogony, 114

Cosmology, 8, 38, 75, 80

Cosmos, 8, 12, 27–30, 72, 74, 76, 77, 84, 85, 87, 88, 94, 100, 172

Crisis, 1–6, 15, 28, 29f., 77, 79, 87

Critical liturgiology, 175

Cross, 36, 39, 40, 43, 46, 57, 62, 97, 163, 216

Cult, 37, 39, 97, 137

Cultural, 2, 7, 9, 10, 11–15, 25, 26, 28, 30, 39–42, 44, 46, 47, 61–63, 65, 72–75, 79, 86, 89, 98, 109, 156f.

Culture, 14, 22, 28, 35, 40, 41, 43, 45, 53, 71, 74, 84, 95, 123, 173f.

Cyclic time, 115, 116

D

Death of Christ, 116, 139, 154–58, 177, 198, 215

Demystification, 25f., 201

Demythologization, 23ff., 28, 110

Domination, 25, 26, 27, 67, 90, 95, 105, 209

Double meaning, 65–67, 79

Doxology, 167

E

Ecclesial, 3, 18, 31, 72

Ecclesiasticism, 18, 19, 25, 26, 27, 90, 93

Eschatology, 20, 30, 38, 40, 78, 202, 215. *See also* Anticipation, Kingdom

230

Imitation, 88, 93, 94, 115, 117, 118, 120, 124
Interiority, 8, 9, 73, 74, 100, 103, 122, 175, 189f.
Interpretation, 2, 26, 36, 37, 43–45, 48, 56, 84, 103f., 172–210

J

Jesus, 36, 37, 39, 65, 67, 70, 97, 112, 120, 121, 125, 131, 136, 198, 201. *See also* Christ, Jesus Christ
Jesus Christ, 1, 3, 13, 14, 20, 27, 30, 31, 35, 36, 37, 38, 39, 42, 43, 44, 48, 70, 97, 103, 114, 115, 119, 120, 122, 145, 146, 154–58, 173, 184, 203, 204, 205, 208, 215, 216. *See also* Christ, Jesus
Jewish, 1, 35, 36, 37, 38, 39, 65, 94, 173
Judaism, 36, 37, 38, 39, 94, 173
Judeo-Christian, 77, 87, 99, 115

K

Kingdom, 16, 31, 38, 78, 120, 123, 125, 126, 130, 132, 136, 139, 209, 210

L

Lamentation, 164–67, 209
Language, *passim*
Limit-situations, 201f.
Liturgy, 144–68, *and passim*

M

Maria Laach, 114, 116
Marriage, 66, 91, 93, 95, 104, 147
Mass, 177
Meaning, 7, 8, 9, 11, 18, 25, 36, 37, 38, 41, 43, 62–68, 70, 72, 73, 75, 80, 82, 85, 86, 91, 96, 97, 98, 102, 103, 105, 108, 128, 132, 173, 186–88, 198f.
Medieval, 18, 49, 50, 51, 57, 101
Memorial, 39, 42, 66, 117, 118, 120–24, 127, 128, 130, 146, 164, 204
Memorial command, 149–52
Memory, 31, 37, 39, 40, 48, 49, 69, 72, 73, 77, 118, 120–24, 127, 130, 202

Psychic, 20, 23, 72, 73, 74, 91, 172
Purification, 44, 50, 90, 91, 97, 99, 101, 102, 103

R

S

Symbolic process, 184–96
Symbolic retrieval, 28–30

T
Testimony, 67, 97, 146, 154–58, 164
Thanksgiving, 41, 46, 91, 117, 126, 137, 164, 167
Theology, 18, 26, 27, 31, 49, 54, 61, 67, 87, 93, 95, 129, 180–
   210
Theophany, 115
Time, temporal, 1, 6, 42, 44, 45, 62, 64, 75, 76, 78, 79, 81, 83,
   85, 87, 95
Transformation, 30, 38, 45, 72, 84, 98, 136, 138, 146f., 184
Truth, 16, 20, 22, 47, 49, 53, 55, 56, 74, 100, 213–16

U
Utopia, 184

V
Value, 7, 14, 15, 24, 30, 62, 63, 68, 69, 70, 72, 75, 80, 89, 98,
   188f., 210
Verbal images, 98–104, *and passim*
Victims, 26, 27, 31, 77, 180, 208, 214
Visual, 42, 52, 57, 79, 98, 175f.

W
Word of God, 16, 48, 49, 77, 78, 115–17, 122, 174
World view, 1, 6, 8, 14, 31, 206–10
Worship, *passim*

PERSONS

A
Amalar of Metz, 52
Ambrose of Milan, 43
Anselm of Canterbury, 154, 211
Aubry, André, 34, 217
Auerbach, Eric, 141, 217
Augustine of Hippo, 48, 49, 56, 59, 61, 138f., 142
Avila, Rafael, 212, 217

235

Duquoc, Christian, 170, 220, 223
Durand, Gilbert, 106, 220

E
Eliade, Mircea, 87, 106, 140, 220
Eliot, T. S., 133f., 143

F
Francis of Assisi, 17, 18
Freud, Sigmund, 33, 73, 162
Frye, Northrop, 21, 33, 141, 220

G
Gadamer, Hans-Georg, 105, 143
Gaiffre, B. de, 142, 220
Gavin, Francis, 57, 220
Geertz, Clifford, 11, 12, 32, 80, 81, 220
Geffré, Claude, 170, 220
Gennep, Arnold Von, 91, 106
Gheerbrant, Alain, 80, 218
Gilkey, Langdon, 81, 220
Gryson, Roger, 59, 221
Guthrie, Harvey, 148, 169, 221
Guzie, Tad, 169, 221

H
Hahn, Ferdinand, 57, 221
Hamerton-Kelly, Robert, 170, 171, 221
Hamman, Adalbert, 58, 221
Happel, Stephen, 171, 221
Hardison, O. B., 60, 221
Häring, N. M., 59, 221
Hart, Ray, 142, 184, 211, 221
Heidegger, Martin, 107, 221
Holeton, David, 59, 221
Hugo of St. Victor, 55, 56
Huizinga, Johan, 84, 105, 222
Hulme, T. E., 133

J

K

L

M

N

O

P

Perrin, Norman, 142, 143, 224
Perrot, Charles, 169, 224
Pius XII, 210
Pohier, Jacques, 170, 224
Power, David N., 106, 211, 214, 223
Pseudo-Dionysius, 18, 48–51, 59

R

Rahner, Karl, 196, 199f., 211, 212, 224
Ricoeur, Paul, 24, 31, 33, 80, 81, 99, 105–7, 140, 142, 143,
    159, 164f., 168, 170, 171, 206, 210, 212, 224, 225
Riley, Hugh M., 59, 140, 225
Rosato, Philip J., 212, 225

S

Schaldenbrand, Mary, 142, 225
Scheer, Anthonius, 142, 225
Schillebeeckx, Edward, 141, 145, 169, 170, 197–99, 200, 201,
    212, 226
Scholes, Robert, 141, 226
Searle, Mark, 212, 226
Segundo, Juan Luis, 33, 226
Smith, Jonathan Z., 58, 226
Spinks, Brian, 58, 226

T

Theodore of Mopsuestia, 43, 52
Thomas Aquinas, 16, 19, 54, 55, 60, 181–83
Tracy, David, 81, 226
Turner, Victor W., 179, 211, 226

V

Vergote, Antoine, 61, 80, 159, 170, 227
Vonier, Anscar, 181, 211, 227

W

Weber, Hans-Ruedi, 57, 227
Westermann, Claus, 171, 227